The Pocket Therapist

The Pocket Therapist

Practical tools to cope with life, relationships and children

Susie Wise
and **Cyndi Kaplan-Freiman**

SIMON & SCHUSTER
AUSTRALIA

The advice given in this book is based on the authors' experience. Professionals should be consulted for individual's problems. The authors and publisher shall not be responsible for any person with regard to any loss or damage caused directly or indirectly by the information in this book.

First published in Australia in 2001 by
Simon & Schuster (Australia) Pty Limited
20 Barcoo Street, East Roseville NSW 2069

A Viacom Company
Sydney New York London Toronto Singapore

National Library of Australia
Cataloguing-in-Publication data

Wise, Susie
The pocket therapist: practical tools to cope with life, relationships and children.

Includes index.
ISBN 0 7318 0982 3.

1. Life skills. 2. Self-help techniques.
I. Kaplan, Cyndi, 1952. II. Title.

158.1

Cover design: Gayna Murphy GREENDOT
Internal design: Avril Makula GRAVITY AAD
Typeset in Sabon 10.5 pt on 14 pt
Printed in Australia by Griffin Press

10 9 8 7 6 5 4 3 2

Contents

section three

PARENTING

Acknowledgments

I have been fortunate to have had many people in my life who have helped me become the person I am and who, in that process, have helped me to write this book.

I would like to thank my mother Lilly, who at 85 is a true role model. She has innate goodness, generosity and love for her family. Her ability to cope with all that has come her way, as well her capacity to enjoy every day as if it were her last, is a real inspiration.

Joe, my late father, came into my life when I was eight years old. He was a true father to me. He was a remarkable man who loved me unconditionally, even when I least deserved it. I will always be grateful for his wisdom and for the confidence he showed in me. He always told me, 'You can do anything you put your mind to'. Only after his death nine years ago did I really appreciate all that he meant to me.

I would also like to thank my wonderful husband Trevor, who has filled my life with love, warmth, generosity, thoughtfulness and understanding. He has helped me grow as a person through his continual support for everything that I undertake. His love for my children and our grandchildren, and the tremendous love and respect he shows my mother, is proof of the special person that he is.

My children, Vivienne and Ronny, are the two most well-adjusted people I know, and are a great source of pride to me. Together with their partners, Grahame and Michele, they have given Trevor and me four fantastic grandchildren – Jessica,

Melissa, Nicholas and Simon – who have helped to make our family complete.

An ex-client of mine, Jo, gave me the most wonderful gift I have ever received – a book she had put together which contained all she had learned from me during our therapy sessions. This thoughtful gift was the inspiration for this book.

Cyndi and I would like to thank Clare Wallis and Jody Lee of Simon & Schuster for their invaluable help and support in the editing process of this book.

Cyndi, without you I would have never taken up this challenge at an age when many are considering retirement. Writing a book had never been one of my ambitions. Your faith in my contribution as a therapist helped me to overcome my reservations. It was something new for both of us. You are such an independent person, and the fact that you have never collaborated on a book before makes this experience even more valuable to me.

We had so much fun and laughter while writing this book. 'Our Tuesdays' always started with lunch and some great laughs before you pushed me to focus on work and deadlines. During this time our friendship, and our love and respect for each other, has grown. Thank you so much for the experience and for reinforcing what my father taught me:

'There is no such thing as can't.'

About the Authors

SUSIE WISE was born in Hungary, and was a child survivor of the Holocaust. She lost her father when she was four. Susie was ten when her family came to Australia, and her mother and step-father worked hard to build a new life. Her early experiences, learning a new language and adapting to a new country, along with subsequent life events, gave her empathy with her clients when she became a therapist. Susie trained as a social worker and worked for eleven years at the Prince of Wales hospital with chronically ill children and their families. She has been in private practice for fourteen years.

Susie's expertise covers individual, couples and teenager therapy, as well as behaviour management of children. She has studied extensively the areas of marital therapy, sexual counselling and behavioural management, and runs groups for parents of children in kindergarten. She is practical, down-to-earth and solution-focused. While understanding a person's history is important, she prefers to work in the 'here and now'.

'If I feel that I am not the best therapist for a problem, such as eating disorders or sexual abuse, I will refer my client to a therapist who specialises in that area. I believe in providing the tools for clients to resolve their own problems – it is up to the individual to use the tools to bring about change.

The therapeutic relationship helps you examine the pros and cons of different actions you may take. You may consider therapy a luxury, but you are actually investing in yourself. I see a therapist as being a caring, objective person who can guide you into making your own decisions.

Why go to a therapist? Sometimes you are not able to share certain issues with family or friends. Friends often tell you what they think you want to hear. Many hidden issues are revealed in therapy, including family secrets such as sexual abuse or domestic violence. For this reason, it is vital that you trust your therapist and that your sessions are confidential.

Susie is passionate about her work, and is committed to helping people improve the quality of their lives. She has an enormous capacity to care, and motivates her clients to work towards solving their own problems. More than a counsellor or a therapist, Susie is a life strategist.

CYNDI KAPLAN-FREIMAN is the author of eight books, including the bestseller *There is a Lipstick in My Briefcase*. She has a degree in psychology and has spent over twenty years in business. She is currently a full-time writer and motivational speaker. Cyndi's email address is: cyndi@bigpond.net.au

Note: In this book, Cyndi interviews Susie and together they explore solutions to problems that we all encounter at some time in our lives. Cyndi's voice is in bold and italics, and Susie's voice is the main text. A number of case studies to illustrate certain concepts have also used; these are clearly indicated.

We have alternated the gender throughout the book to avoid any stereotyping except where a specific gender is clearly appropriate. In all cases names have been changed to protect the identity of the clients. Most stories are composites, combinations of different experiences.

Introduction

When we have a medical problem, we consult a doctor. When the problem is emotional, we may need to seek help from a psychotherapist. However, some of us find it difficult to reveal our thoughts and feelings to a stranger. We may find it painful to confront our inner turmoil and vulnerability, or we may feel ashamed to seek help. There is still a stigma attached to the idea of not being able to cope alone, as if asking for help is a sign of weakness. But this attitude prevents us from receiving the help we need.

In recent years, our lives have become more complex and our families more fragmented. Many of us are not surrounded by close friends or trusted family members, and so may need outside help in times of crisis. And an objective outsider can often help us gain insight or skills to solve our problems.

The aim of this book is to give you a taste of what you may experience in the therapeutic situation. Hopefully it will demystify the process of therapy and encourage you to seek professional help in dealing with some of life's greater challenges. We have divided this book into three sections: The Self, Relationships and Parenting. The rationale behind this structure is that in order to be ready for a healthy, functional relationship we need to deal with our personal issues first. For example, someone with low self-esteem may struggle in relationships if they expect that the other person can provide them with what they lack in themselves. This rarely happens. By working through your own issues, you will be more likely to have happy and fulfilling relationships with others, be it a partner, friends or work colleagues.

In a similar way, in order to be an effective parent, we need to become aware of our own issues and work through them. If we do not do this, we are likely to repeat these mistakes or unhealthy patterns with our children.

Someone once told me that the best thing parents can ever do for their children is to love each other. As parents we are modelling a relationship to our children. If children are exposed to an abusive, violent or dysfunctional marriage, it will leave a deep imprint on them.

As you can see, the three areas feed into each other. The self is not a static entity. It is affected by changes in our life: losses, stresses, career ups and downs, health and many other variables. What we do need are tools and strategies to deal with these changes in our life. So by investing in ourselves, we are also paving the way for happier relationships and more effective parenting.

There are many different kinds of therapy. Some people respond more positively to one approach than the other but when you choose a therapist, don't worry too much about the approach or method. The most important aspect of therapy is that you feel relaxed, comfortable and safe. As Carl Rogers has said, 'There are four basic requirements of therapy: warmth, empathy, genuineness and positive regard for the client.'

It may take more than one session to find out whether you are happy with your therapist. If it doesn't feel right, ask around. Get referrals and try someone else. But when you find someone you are happy with, the experience can be a life-changing one.

You will gain the most value out of your sessions if you see them as an opportunity to learn skills. Go along with a notebook and pen. Be prepared to work. Ask questions and write down important concepts. The duration of therapy depends on the effort you are prepared to invest and how willing you are to learn. Before you embark on a series of sessions with your chosen therapist, you may like to ask the cost of each session, how many sessions your therapist anticipates would be needed to treat your problem and what approach will be used – cognitive, behavioural, narrative or eclectic, or a combination of different styles.

Here are some tips for getting the most out of your sessions with a therapist:

- Book a regular session time each week, and arrange it so that you don't have to rush back to work. You may feel you need a little time to gather your thoughts together and settle your feelings.
- Don't be late. Make sure you arrive in good time.
- Make sure your therapist maintains confidentiality.
- Don't feel compelled to discuss your therapy sessions with friends, or even your partner, until you feel ready, or ever. You are entitled to keep your sessions personal and private.
- Keep your relationship with your therapist on a professional level only. This creates formal boundaries.
- Choose someone close to your office or home, so that traffic and distance do not become a deterrent to continuing therapy.
- Choose someone most suited to your kind of problem. For example, if you have suffered the death of a loved one, go to a bereavement therapist. If your marriage is in trouble go to a relationship expert. If you need help with your children, find a therapist who is skilled in behaviour management. Do your research and you are more likely to find the appropriate person. Ask your doctor, school counsellor or friends for referrals or look in the Yellow Pages.

Susie's Dedication

I dedicate this book to my mother Lilly and my late father Joe, who taught me:

'When somebody asks, you give,
And while you give,
Thank God that you are in a position to give
And that you are not the one needing to ask.'

section one

The **Self**

We have chosen to start the book by looking at aspects of the self. These aspects connect and overlap. For example, self-esteem is affected by depression, stress and anger. In order to have healthy relationships, avoid stress and create firm boundaries, we need positive self-esteem. It is therefore important to look at ourselves before looking at our relationships.

Building healthy self-esteem will give you the confidence to communicate more assertively, create firm boundaries with others, and manage your time so that you suffer less stress. Positive self-worth will help you build resistance to depression. Repressed anger may also lead to depression. Learning how to get in touch with your anger, express your feelings and deal with them constructively is healthier than suppressing your emotions.

We all experience loss at different times of our life. For most of us, it is a traumatic event – the death of a loved one, divorce, relationship breakdown or loss of youth, good health or a job. Loss has an impact on our self-worth and therefore on how we see ourselves. When someone we love dies, we lose a part of ourselves and need to mourn the loss before we can rebuild our lives effectively. In our Western culture, the grieving process is often repressed. By having an understanding of the grief process we can go through the pain knowing that it is a stage, and that it will, and should, end.

Being able to communicate effectively is the touchstone of all our relationships. Our ability to have our needs met within those relationships depends on successful communication patterns. By understanding our own communication style, we gain insight into how we interact with others and why they respond the way they do. If you discover you are locked into negative communication patterns and this is why you are experiencing conflict with others, you can use the tools provided to make positive changes.

All these facets of the self overlap and interconnect. Insight and life skills in each of these areas will help you build a stronger sense of self. This, in turn, will put you in a position to have more satisfying relationships and become a more effective parent.

chapter one

Understanding Self-Esteem

DANI IS THE THIRTY-EIGHT-YEAR-OLD MOTHER of two sons, aged seven and nine. She had been married for ten years when her marriage ended. She shares her story.

When my husband Steve left me for my best friend, I was devastated. For over a year, I had suspected that he was having an affair, but each time I confronted him about it, he would deny it and accuse me of being paranoid. He would bash me, kick me, or in some way abuse me. He made me feel as if I was going mad. I had no-one to turn to as my family lived abroad. On many nights I cried myself to sleep in the spare room.

After ten years with Steve, my self-esteem was shattered. I felt stupid, incompetent, and unable to cope. Then he left, and after all the years of abuse, I just fell apart. I couldn't eat, I couldn't sleep. I couldn't leave the home and I couldn't look after my children. I was terrified of being alone, so eventually my GP and our minister decided I should be checked into a nursing home where I could be looked after.

I was there for two weeks. I was seen by a psychiatrist and attended group therapy sessions. I was put on anti-depressant medication. But when I came home, I still didn't feel well enough to cope. I was tearful, depressed and lacked the motivation to create a life for myself. I couldn't find the energy to do ordinary things such as shop, look after my children, or even get dressed. Luckily, a wonderful friend came to the rescue and insisted on taking me out for walks. He helped me get a part-time job and I gradually gained strength and confidence.

It's now four years since that traumatic episode. I had an extended period of therapy. This gave me both insight into myself and coping skills. I realised that I had allowed my ex-husband to undermine my self-esteem. With my share of the divorce settlement, I bought a small semi, which I renovated. I love my home. I have also started a small business, which is going well, and I am in a special relationship.

My outlook on life has changed. Small things don't upset me any more. Although there are tough moments, the important thing to remember is that I am out of an abusive relationship, and I am so much stronger, more confident and enjoying my independence. I hardly feel the same woman who fell apart when my husband left me.

This story reveals how our self-esteem can be eroded by an abusive relationship. Once Dani was free of her destructive relationship, she sought professional help and was able to heal. Self-esteem comes from the Latin word *estimo* meaning 'I value'. It relates to the value you place on yourself. If you feel good about who you are, you may describe yourself as having high self-esteem. If you lack confidence you are more likely to have low self-esteem. We all need the precious attribute of self-esteem to enhance the quality of our lives and have healthy relationships.

High self-esteem gives you a sense of being worthwhile, and enables you to feel satisfied with life. You are more likely to love yourself and create good relationships with others. You will be assertive and ensure that your needs are met in relationships.

You will also have a sense of control over your life. Part of this control is the ability to say 'no' without guilt, to set boundaries on your space, and to use your time to achieve the things that are important to you. High self-esteem allows you to be self-directed, to trust yourself to take on fresh challenges, and to have the confidence that you will succeed with new projects.

If you have low self-esteem, you may be consumed with negative thoughts. You fear new experiences and find it hard to make new friends or to take on responsibility. You will most likely spend your life trying to please others instead of doing what you want, resulting in a feeling of resentment.

Susie will explain how we acquire self-esteem and how to turn a negative self-image into a positive one.

Can you explain how our self-esteem develops?

For most of us, self-esteem has its roots in the way we were parented and the emotional environment of our home. Every child comes into the world with his own personality, needs and attributes. This uniqueness needs to be respected.

A child needs unconditional love in order to develop positive self-esteem. He needs to feel he is loved for who he is, rather than for what he does or achieves. If a child is criticised constantly, deprived of affection, or rejected by his parents, he grows up believing he is not worthwhile. Constant emotional battering and abuse, be it physical, sexual or psychological, further damages self-esteem.

Parents don't set out to deprive children of love deliberately. Sometimes their own low self-esteem means they are unable to give their children emotional security and affection. This cycle then perpetuates itself. The good news is that it is never too late to develop positive self-esteem. By becoming aware of our situation, we can learn to nurture and strengthen our self-esteem as adults. We can reverse the damage.

What are some further signs that a person may have low self-esteem?

He may consistently predict failure for himself, which becomes a self-fulfilling prophecy. He is likely to go into a relationship feeling that when his partner gets to know him, she will not like him any more. In these situations, what you fear most is exactly what happens. On the other hand, if you go into a situation expecting a positive outcome, this is usually what happens. Failure fuels low self-esteem in the same way that success enhances positive self-esteem.

Can you say a little more about how low self-esteem affects personal relationships?

If you have low self-esteem, you are in danger of attracting someone with low self-esteem. If you have continual negative thoughts, if you are very severe on yourself, critical of all that you are and do, and if you often ask yourself, 'What have I done' or 'Have I done something wrong?', you may take on responsibility for things that are not your fault in a relationship. If your partner is also doing this, it is likely to be an unhappy relationship.

You cannot depend on someone else to make you feel good. This is something that comes from within. I always discourage people from getting into relationships in the early stages of therapy. Chances are they would choose someone different after therapy.

GROW AN INCH

WHEN YOU ARE LACKING CONFIDENCE, PRETEND A STRING IS ATTACHED TO YOUR HEAD AND IT IS PULLING YOU UP. YOU WILL INSTANTLY LOOK AND FEEL AN INCH TALLER. PUT YOUR SHOULDERS BACK, PUT A SMILE ON YOUR FACE AND MAKE EYE CONTACT WITH PEOPLE. YOU WILL SEEM THE MOST CONFIDENT PERSON IN THE ROOM.

Can you lose your self-esteem once you have it?

Self-esteem is not a fixed quality; it is an ongoing process that goes through change and development. As we go through life, we may have experiences that challenge our self-esteem. These include relationship break-ups, illness, the death of someone close, losing a job, moving to another location, even ageing. Learning skills to nurture your self-esteem will enable you to pick yourself up when you get knocked about.

We each have our own pattern of responding to life events, so if we have strong, positive self-esteem, we are likely to bounce back more quickly when something stressful happens. Healthy self-esteem is, to a large extent, dependent on our ability to cope with change in our life and retain a feeling of self-worth.

What other changes affect our self-esteem?

Loss has an impact on self-esteem. It could be the loss of a job through redundancy or the loss of a woman's looks as she ages. Some cope with losses graciously; others suffer depression. We will deal with loss more extensively in Chapter 3.

Another danger time for women is when their children have grown and no longer need taking care of. If being a homemaker was your main role, then the feeling of loss when your children leave home can be tremendous. It is also wise to prepare for the time you retire from the workplace so that you are not left with a feeling of emptiness. Prepare for this phase of your life by developing outside interests such as hobbies and charitable work.

In order to cope with losses in life, self-esteem must be based on a solid foundation. For this we need to gain an inner strength. This will give us a real feeling of self-worth that is not based on approval of others. We all need to belong to family, friends and a community, but we need inner strength to cope with losses in any of these areas. Being overly dependent on others can lead to a crisis in self-esteem that will help to diminish this inner strength.

Be easy on yourself. Remember that only the people who never take risks or who don't accept new challenges end up not making mistakes. This may be a safe path but you will not grow, or develop your self-confidence or self-worth if you avoid change and new challenges.

Can you suggest some ways to strengthen shaky self-esteem?

There are some simple self-esteem exercises to start with. I suggest taking a pen and paper, and making a list of all your positive attributes, skills and accomplishments. Sing your own praises. So often we focus on what we perceive to be our negative qualities or shortcomings. You may be a fabulous cook, or you may enjoy gardening. Write these things down. For the next two weeks, add one new quality to your list every day. You will be amazed at how many positive qualities you can find about yourself. By focusing on the positives you will start feeling better about yourself.

Another exercise you can do to enhance your self-esteem is to make a list of your priorities every day. Slot in a time for the activities you have given priority to and give yourself permission to protect the time you have allocated to them. Value your time and only give it away when you feel the requests are worthwhile. When you accomplish what you have set for yourself, you feel a sense of satisfaction. When day after day you only do things others ask of you, you may feel dissatisfied, and your self-esteem will be affected.

We need to create an emotional environment for ourselves that allows our self-esteem to flourish. We have the power to give our children positive self-esteem also, so this same environment should provide our children with love and affection, respect and an encouragement to express their feelings. Children need to feel safe so that they can share their feelings without being judged, rejected or punished.

LARA, AGED 27, STARTED COMING to see me after she realised that a recent failed relationship had been very abusive. She shared her feelings:

I realise I have a lot of self-esteem issues. My older sister is very bright. When I was a child, my parents were very critical of everything I did. They gave me no encouragement whatsoever. They would say, 'You are stupid', 'What do you know', or 'Who do you think you are?' I have always found it difficult to accept any compliments. I feel I have no sense of self. I am whatever someone else wants me to be, so I never feel truly myself.

I'm emotionally exhausted from trying to please everybody else. I no longer know who I am. I don't seem able to maintain a relationship. I seem to choose men who are very abusive. I feel lost, isolated and alone. My father was always particularly critical of me. As a result I'm overly critical of myself. I blame myself when things don't turn out well. I'm tired of fighting with this very unforgiving part of myself. I question whether I'm a good person. I feel guilty if I don't visit my parents when they invite me. I feel unattractive and have a negative self-image.

We began a series of sessions, the aim of which was for Lara to discover her positive attributes. We then looked at changes she wanted to make in her behaviour. We examined her short-term goals and her long-term aspirations and gradually started to work towards her achieving some of these. I suggested that Lara should take up some new interests and learn skills that would give her self-confidence. She chose to enroll in a pottery class and a yoga course. Both activities gave her an opportunity to learn something different, be creative and meet new friends.

She enrolled in a TAFE course, and success in that field proved a boost to her self-esteem. One of her goals was to help others. She loved working with children, so she decided to go once a week to the children's hospital to play with children who come to Australia from disadvantaged countries for medical treatment. Many of them come without family, so they have no visitors. This helped lift Lara's spirit and gave her a feeling of being important to others. She gradually began to believe in herself, make positive changes and focus less on her negative feelings.

What is the connection between self-esteem and self-confidence?

Self-esteem and self-confidence go hand in hand. If you are self-confident, you are more willing to take risks and tackle new projects. This could be something as simple as planting a vegetable garden or doing a cookery course. Self-confidence grows as we experience trust in ourselves to take on new challenges. We can give ourselves permission to have a go without needing to be perfect.

In my work teaching art to children, I see many children who are afraid to start to draw in case they make a mistake. The white paper in front of them is threatening. I encourage them to begin. I remind them that learning involves many attempts and that each try is progress in the effort to express themselves. As soon as they begin, they gain confidence.

When I began public speaking, I lacked confidence. I was very nervous. My knees would shake, my hands would be clammy and I would have butterflies raging in my tummy. Gradually I became more relaxed, until I actually started to enjoy the process. After many presentations the anxiety evaporated and I began to enjoy public speaking. The only way to deal with the fear is to face it and move through it. Go through the field of fear and into the field of confidence. Confidence only builds into more confidence.

Self-esteem works from the inside out. It is based on what is within you and how closely your outer life reflects your inner qualities and values. As you accept and respect yourself more, you will give yourself the gift of positive self-esteem. Another building block of self-esteem is assertiveness. I believe that in every relationship, we have a lot more control than we think in terms of how that relationship will progress.

Can you explain further?

There are three ways of relating to people. Firstly, a non-assertive style, where you can't tell people what you really want. You give in to others. Secondly, an aggressive style, where you need to control others and have your own way, and thirdly, an assertive style, which is the most desirable mode of being.

When you are assertive, you respect your own rights and the rights of others. You show respect for the other person and yourself. You can talk about your feelings and actions. You don't blame others. When you are being assertive, your tone of voice, body language and the way you phrase things project confidence. When you are assertive, you are comfortable saying 'no', and you are honest about what your needs are.

Non-assertive people fear being honest in case they hurt other people's feelings. They fear they will not be liked. They avoid blame and responsibility by leaving choices to others. They fear being rejected. At worst they can be martyrs. They often feel hard done by and resentful for always giving in or putting other people's needs first.

One of my clients, Bella, has three children and five grandchildren. She is often asked to babysit. She feels that if she gives time to one set of grandchildren, she must give time to the others. She wants to please so much that she never refuses. She puts off doing what she really wants to do because of pressure to please her children and grandchildren. She came to see me as she was feeling resentful towards her family. She felt used. She was suppressing her own needs. I advised her to look at her own needs. We role-played a situation in which she could say 'no' in an assertive but warm, caring way to one of her children's babysitting requests: 'I would love to babysit but I have other plans'.

Bella realised that the world would not come to an end if she said 'no'. We then planned that every fourth time she was asked to do something in the family she would refuse. We rehearsed the scene: 'I know you'd really like me to do this for you and I wish I could but I have other commitments'. This worked very well. She was able to balance time for her own social life with enjoyable time babysitting her grandchildren. It took a while for her to feel comfortable saying 'no', but soon all her feelings of resentment towards her family disappeared. Her daughter told her how pleased she was that her mum was finally doing some activities she enjoyed with her friends. The rejection or resentment from her children never came.

What's the pay-off for being non-assertive?

In the short-term, non-assertive people avoid conflict; they keep the peace in order to be liked, but in the end they become resentful. Practise expressing discontent using the 'I' message. For example, 'When you did that, I felt the following'. If you are a non-assertive person, write down a list of areas where you could assert yourself in a range of relationships. Create a list in order from the least difficult to the hardest. When an occasion arises, practise assertive behaviour. This does not mean you have to be aggressive. Here is an example:

PEOPLE SPEND TIME WITH PEOPLE WHO MAKE THEM FEEL GOOD ABOUT THEMSELVES

IF A RELATIONSHIP IS NOT GOING WELL, ASK YOURSELF IF YOU ARE A PLEASURE TO BE AROUND. ARE YOU TOO CRITICAL? ARE YOU OVER-SENSITIVE? IS IT HARD WORK TO HAVE A RELATIONSHIP WITH YOU? COULD YOU BE MORE EASY-GOING? IT'S UP TO YOU HOW YOU BEHAVE.

Amanda and Jamie have been married for three years. They were experiencing marital problems due to poor communication skills. Jamie had difficulty controlling his anger. Although he was not physically abusive, he was verbally abusive to Amanda. Her reaction was to withdraw in order to avoid any further conflict. Amanda found these episodes very frightening. She was afraid to express her feelings as she thought this may escalate his reactions. She felt she could only do one of two things: be defensive or withdraw emotionally.

One day Amanda kept Jamie waiting for five minutes after being delayed at work by her boss. By the time she got to the car James was seething with fury. He lost his temper without giving her a chance to explain what had happened.

Amanda came to me to discuss the problem. I suggested to her that next time an incident occurred, she should wait till he had calmed down, then say to him, 'I know you're upset that I'm late. Rather than become angry and say hurtful things, I would really appreciate if you didn't speak to me that way'.

Amanda was amazed at how willing Jamie was to listen, and to her surprise, he apologised for his bad temper. This positive experience gave Amanda the willpower to handle future situations in a more assertive way.

When you are continually non-assertive or passive you feel like a victim. The more assertive you become, the more you will be able to express your feelings and feel in control of your life. Assertive behaviour is needed in all situations: at work, with family, parenting and in your relationship with friends.

Another aspect of assertive behaviour involves having clear boundaries, protecting your personal space and managing your time so that you are doing what you want to do. Don't confuse assertiveness with selfishness. Make sure that your own feelings or needs receive equal priority with the needs of others.

Aggressive people usually lack self-esteem and are insecure. They mask their feelings of inadequacy by behaving in an aggressive manner. They may be critical, blame others, use sarcasm or withdraw into silence. Aggressive people may try to dominate or control others in order to feel good about themselves. You may be expressing aggressive behaviour yourself or you may recognise you are in a relationship with an aggressive person. This can have a detrimental effect on your self-esteem as the aggressive person tries to put you down, constantly criticising your behaviour. Aggressive people mask their own low self-esteem by bullying others.

What are other killers of healthy self-esteem?

Maybe I can best answer you with an example:

Sandra, a young woman of twenty-five, came to see me because she needed help. She wanted to experience more pleasure in her life. She was lonely, had no friends and any relationship she had only lasted a few weeks. She had low self-esteem and felt very down, although she was not clinically depressed. Looking back on her life she had difficulty remembering any happy moments.

Sandra had a younger sister whom she perceived as prettier than her. Her parents worked hard and did not ever go out to enjoy themselves. On weekends they sat at home and watched television. They were often critical of Sandra as a child. She therefore tended to have a negative disposition and was quick to blame others if things did not work out. She also begrudged others what they had. She felt inadequate and was rejected by others. She became a loner. She was also super-sensitive and reactive. This made others wary of connecting with her.

After a few sessions it became evident that Sandra's feelings of inadequacy and inferiority were unwarranted. She was brighter than she gave herself credit for and she could look attractive if she applied a little make-up and wore more flattering clothes. After three months of therapy, she was well on the way to developing a more positive perception of herself. She enrolled in an advanced computer course, which led directly to a better job in her company. She became involved in charity work and this involvement added to her confidence.

I asked Sandra to keep a daily journal in which she wrote down situations that she found difficult to handle. I gradually showed her how to change her reactions to situations and how she related to others. We role-played various situations so that she could have the opportunity of stepping into the shoes of someone else. I always played her in these scenarios.

Gradually her attitude became more positive and she learnt how to smile more often and look people in the eye when she spoke to them. She accepted compliments graciously and gave positive feedback to others. She attended a make-up course and learnt how to apply make-up in a way that enhanced her features. We looked at fashion magazines and chose a few outfits that we thought would suit her. She gradually made more friends and improved her self-image.

How can we cope with feelings of guilt?

Guilt can damage self-esteem. We all do things from time to time that we regret, or have an error of judgement. However, general guilt, whereby we condemn ourselves for who we are, can be very painful and destructive. We may develop strong feelings of guilt if we were brought up with statements such as: 'I'm ashamed of you' or 'I'm disappointed in you'. If you suffer from a sense of guilt, try to find the source of this feeling.

When we have low self-esteem, we often accept blame for things that go wrong. For example, apologising for choosing a movie that your partner did not enjoy. If the guilt refers to a traumatic experience in the past, such as sexual abuse, go for professional help.

How do we overcome resentment?

Resentment creates tension in our lives and lowers our self-esteem. We often become resentful if we suppress our anger or feelings of unfairness. Unfinished business from the past has a way of reappearing, nagging at us, demanding attention and solutions. We must therefore deal with issues as they arise. Once we forgive ourselves and others, we release the resentment. When anger is not dealt with, it raises its ugly head when we least expect it.

When there is an issue, it is better to sit down with the other person and sort it out. Explain that there is an issue that you are upset about. Share your feelings and then allow the other person to express his thoughts and feelings. Try to find a solution to the problem.

How do we go about forgiving someone for past hurts?

Forgiveness has two purposes. First of all, it can heal your pain. Secondly, it can repair a damaged relationship. Many people, including our parents, may hurt us unintentionally. As adults we have the capacity to understand this, forgive them and move on. If the person who hurt you is no longer alive, consider writing a letter to them. Express all the pain and anger that their actions caused you. Then burn the letter. By getting in touch with the feelings connected to that person, you may experience a release of blocked emotions.

In forgiving someone, you do not have to approve of his actions. Certain behaviour is never acceptable. However, forgiveness is a willingness to understand and to let go. This process will set you free from hurt, anger, guilt and layers of pain.

Toolbox

- Become your own best friend.
- Spend quality time with yourself. Learn to enjoy your own company.
- Learn to say 'no' without feeling guilty. You are entitled to value and protect your own time.
- Become self-reliant and less needy of others.
- Learn assertive communication skills.
- Connect with positive people and thoughts.
- Challenge yourself to take risks and do different things.
- Learn to look inside yourself for answers to problems.
- Listen at least twice as much as you talk.
- Don't compare yourself with others. Find positive role models.

chapter two

Coping with Anxiety and Depression

NATALIE IS AN ATTRACTIVE, TALENTED nineteen-year-old university student, studying social work. Two years ago, she experienced a deep depression. She is now well, is studying, seeing her friends, and has resumed a full and busy life. She shares her painful experience of depression:

I felt hopeless and helpless. I did not want to get out of bed in the morning. I wanted to sleep all the time. I felt as if my thought processes had slowed down. I did not enjoy my usual activities. Life felt grey and dark, and my self-esteem was low. I felt as if my life lacked purpose and meaning. I didn't want to be around my friends.

My GP recommended me to a therapist, Susie. She helped me to plan activities and create some structure in my life. She suggested that I was up and dressed by nine. I should then go for a walk, phone a friend, and do some uni work or study. I had to have some concrete plans in place. If not, one day looked like the next, without a goal or purpose.

My GP also suggested I take anti-depressants. I resisted at first, and it took a while before I found one that worked for me. I don't think everyone who is depressed needs medication. You need professional guidance to help you decide whether medication is appropriate for you. You can obtain this from your GP or psychiatrist. Regular exercise helped me to recover when I was feeling depressed.

Gradually, with a combination of medication and weekly therapy sessions with Susie, I began to feel better. I have definitely become a stronger person. I have more insight and a greater empathy with others. At the time of my depression, I felt very isolated. I remember thinking, 'Why is this happening to me?' It seemed important to find a reason, but in the end it doesn't matter. What counts is how you deal with it and how you manage yourself. I believe that you get depressed when you have lost meaning and direction in your life. If you can get moving again, physically, mentally and spiritually, you are on the way to healing.

The most frightening part of my depression was the feeling that there was no light at the end of the tunnel. If someone can make you see that there is an end in sight, you will feel better. While you are in a dark depression, it feels like it will never end. Therapy and medication can speed up the healing process and give you coping skills and insight into the experience.

Emotional disorders, one of which is depression, are complex states that often combine a number of elements. There may be a genetic, biochemical or psychological component. There may also be a trigger, such as childbirth, the death of someone close, a viral infection or severe stress.

Depression varies in length of time and intensity. As most depressions, if left untreated, may last from several months to a few years, it is dangerous to ignore them. There is the danger of suicide, and depression is also very difficult for other family members to handle. A person with depression needs treatment and support. It is best to seek professional help as early as possible.

Recovery from depression may take a zig-zag course. Some days the depressed person may seem improved and then the next day they may experience a setback. The key is to make sure the depressed person receives help and is not left to suffer alone or unnecessarily.

Emotional pain is difficult to understand. Family and friends may become impatient with the depressed person. The best thing to do is to encourage her to remain involved in her usual activities, or schedule new ones, even if she is only going through the motions. Physical exercise and more activities are said to improve self-concept and lift our moods. As much as the depressed person resists going out, she will frequently admit that she feels better when involved in pleasurable activities.

According to Dr Kristina Downing-Orr, an expert in the field of depression, ten per cent of the population is seeking help for a mood disorder at any given time. Depression has become the fourth most common health problem that doctors are presented with, and in the past few years there has been a huge increase in the use of anti-depressant drugs. In 2000, in Australia alone, there were over a million prescriptions filled for Prozac and Zoloft, which are the two most popular anti-depressant drugs available.

Schools are introducing programs to make students aware of the early signs and symptoms of depression. Prevention is a major part of this program. Some of the major causes of depression for teenagers include:

- drug abuse;
- problems in the peer group;
- family and school environment;
- genetic predisposition that can be influenced by drugs;
- the teenager being prone to anxiety and worry; and
- eating disorders such as anorexia or bulimia.

In young adults, the same influences prevail, but added to them are the stresses of career success, self-esteem and the ability to form meaningful relationships. From the age of forty onwards, depression may be caused by the onset of health problems, financial worries and relationship breakdown. Later, another vulnerable period emerges when children leave home, and women go through menopause. Understanding some of the life events that predispose a person to depression enables us to give people support when they are most vulnerable.

Despite its prevalence, depression, and the impact it can have on a person's career, relationships and well-being, is often not understood. Indeed, many depressed people do not seek out appropriate help. What we are aiming to do is explain how to recognise the signs of depression and advise you of the spectrum of treatments available.

Certain kinds of depression can be effectively treated with medication. There are a wide variety of anti-depressant drugs available. Therapy can be used to complement drug treatment or, in certain cases, be used instead of medication. To overcome depression, one needs both patience and persistence. Medication takes a few weeks to be effective, and the same applies to therapy.

There is a prevailing myth that people suffering from depression should be able to cope alone and get themselves out of it. Men in particular are often more reluctant to seek help and may resort to alcohol and drugs as a means of escape. It is not a sign of character weakness or moral flaw to become depressed. There is no value in blaming yourself. This only makes the depression worse. In this chapter, we will look at self-management techniques that may prevent you from sinking into a full-blown depression.

What is depression? What does it 'look like'?

Depression exists on a continuum. We all have days when we feel a bit blue. It may be from sadness related to a specific event, or we may be premenstrual or just feeling out of sorts. This feeling usually passes, and after a few days we bounce back to our normal selves. However, if these feelings persist for an extended period of time, we may be entering a full-blown depression. Here are some symptoms to look out for:

- You feel like crying for no reason.
- You are losing or gaining weight.
- You are experiencing sleep disturbances.
- You have persistent feelings of emptiness.

- You lack confidence.
- You feel bad about yourself.
- You feel restless or agitated.
- You feel out of control, vulnerable and helpless.
- You feel you have lost your zest for life.
- Your concentration may deteriorate.
- Your mind may feel heavy or clouded.
- You may feel suicidal.

If some or all of these symptoms describe how you are feeling, do not hesitate to get professional help. The sooner you treat depression, the better. If someone close to you is experiencing these symptoms, do your best to encourage them to seek appropriate help. Sometimes a depressed person may not be motivated to get help because they are feeling so down.

Some people stop eating when they become severely depressed, and may turn to drugs and alcohol for respite. They often withdraw socially and are unable to pay their bills or do their work well. They may also take little care with their appearance.

What are the causes of depression?

The reasons people become depressed vary enormously. Some of us may become depressed for no apparent reason. Certain critical life events may trigger depression – the death of someone close, divorce or the breakdown of a significant relationship, having a baby, moving countries or cities, losing a job, financial loss, or a childhood trauma such as physical, emotional or sexual abuse. You might feel that your life has no purpose, direction or meaning. You may need to look at what is missing in your life in order to identify the problem. You may need to make some lifestyle changes that would give your life more meaning. It is unlikely that one risk factor alone would trigger depression. There is also a genetic component to depression, and therefore some people possess a biological predisposition to becoming depressed. But there are many risk factors, as well as vulnerable times in our lives, that can bring on a bout of depression.

Depression also occurs when a person suppresses anger and turns it inwards. A depressed person may find it difficult to access her anger. The role of the therapist is to help put her in touch with those angry feelings. Poor social skills or a lack of connection to others may also cause loneliness and depression. This isolation and disconnection is illustrated in Paul's story.

PAUL, AGED THIRTY-ONE, CAME TO see me feeling depressed. His GP had put him on a course of anti-depressant medication, but had suggested he go to regular psychotherapy sessions as well. When he first came to me, he was having trouble sleeping, eating and concentrating. He had lost motivation in his job and found it difficult to form meaningful relationships.

We had weekly sessions over a four-month period. Initially, Paul was very lethargic, negative, anxious and miserable. We created an action plan to gradually integrate him into a more active lifestyle. He started with small tasks like washing his car, going for a run, and planning one activity with his friends each week. We drew up a timetable for him to follow so that he had some structure in his life. I gradually encouraged him to delay quitting his job, which he did not particularly like, until he had emerged from the depression. He did later apply for another position and was able to change his work situation.

Susie focused on changing my behaviour, my thoughts and feelings. It was vital to get me moving, motivated and involved in the world again. With the help of medication and therapy, I emerged a stronger person. My depression lifted, leaving me with greater insight and a healthier self-image. Part of my therapy included doing something for someone else every day. This gave me great satisfaction and made me realise that there were other people in the world going through challenging times.

Is anxiety linked to depression? How does anxiety affect our life?

Many people with depression also experience an anxiety disorder. Often the symptoms of anxiety occur before the depression sets in. This suggests that anxiety may well contribute to depression; however, anxiety is an emotional problem in its own right.

Anxiety is common, and millions of people suffer from it to varying degrees. Of course, certain situations can cause a degree of anxiety, such as an examination, job interview or surgery; or the anxiety may be in response to a bigger event such as a wedding or a significant change in a person's life. Some people are naturally more highly strung, or may have a genetic predisposition to being anxious, but often, ongoing anxiety stems from illogical and self-defeating thoughts, which need to be addressed.

Panic attacks are often a manifestation of anxiety. Someone suffering a panic or anxiety attack may experience excessive worry, fear, panic, terror, nausea, a choking feeling, stomach pains, a dry mouth, chest tightness, trembling or shaking, diarrhoea or constipation, clenched teeth and generalised nervousness. Many symptoms of anxiety are extremely disabling. However, there are techniques you can learn to manage your anxiety.

What's the best way to treat anxiety or panic attacks?

People who have panic attacks experience sudden episodes of intense anxiety, often occurring at unexpected moments. The person may even think they are having a heart attack. If you are suffering from severe anxiety attacks, it is best to see a psychologist who specialises in the treatment of anxiety and panic attacks. Treatment would include a combination of medication and psychotherapy. Be aware that certain medications may lead to dependency if not supported with counselling or therapy.

If you suffer from anxiety attacks, you may find some of these suggestions helpful:

- ❖ Don't try to fight the anxiety attack.
- ❖ Do some deep breathing when you start to feel anxious.
- ❖ Focus on the present by becoming aware of your senses – colour, smell, touch and sight. Instead of focusing on the fear, bring yourself into the present moment by asking yourself, 'What am I feeling?'
- ❖ You may feel as if you are going to die. Ask yourself, 'Is there any evidence that I may die?' These thoughts may ground you and stop you from imagining worst-case scenarios. People don't die from panic attacks.
- ❖ Write down a goal you would like to achieve to overcome the anxiety. Break it down into small steps. Take one step at a time. Reward yourself at each victory.
- ❖ Physical exercise, yoga and visualisation exercises will also help you to manage your anxiety. This is a more pro-active approach, and empowers the individual to do something rather than to be dependent on tranquillisers.

I had an interesting experience recently where I had to cope with a situation that provoked a severe panic reaction in me. A group of us was walking along the Milford Track in New Zealand and we had to cross a swinging bridge high over a river. As I am terrified of heights, I was ready to turn back at this moment. I was consumed by terror. My body went into the typical flight/fight reaction. My knees turned to jelly, my mouth went dry and I could not see myself walking across. All the others in the group had crossed. I was the only one frozen by my fear.

Then I talked to myself firmly. Are you going to be paralysed by your fear or move through it? I stepped onto the bridge and filled my mind with positive thoughts only. 'You will get across. Focus on moving your feet. Don't stop, and walk slowly.' Step by step I edged across until I could see I was more than halfway. At this point I experienced a huge surge of confidence which gave me the energy to get to the end of the bridge. When we had to cross other bridges during the walk, I gained confidence and my fear was reduced.

What about stress – how does that relate to depression?

As our lives become more complex, our stress levels increase. Many of us juggle a multitude of roles, and stress occurs when we feel frustration, pressure or guilt around these different demands. We also experience stress as a response to traumatic life events such as financial problems, divorce, illness and other big changes. Most of us experience ups and downs as we go through the journey of life but if we don't learn to manage stress in our lives, it may turn into depression. In order to deal with whatever life has to offer, we need to develop coping skills and survival tactics.

What are some of these strategies?

The most powerful antidote to depression is a positive attitude. It is important to allow yourself to feel sad after a loss or painful experience, but an optimistic outlook will help you deal positively with the pain. If you feel yourself moving beyond sadness into despair you need to see a good therapist. Besides reading positive books and connecting with caring friends, a therapist can help you manage your feelings, which may seem out of control. A therapist will give you objective insight into your depression and help you identify your fears.

Which is more effective in treating depression and anxiety, anti-depressants or therapy?

In most cases, a combination of the two will be most effective. Therapists and psychologists use talk therapy, as they are not permitted to prescribe medication. If you have severe depression, you may need some medication before you will benefit from counselling or therapy. Your GP or a psychiatrist can prescribe suitable medication.

In my practice, I have a few sessions with the client and assess their level of anxiety or depression using a questionnaire. If the result indicates that the person is severely depressed, or seems unable to carry out certain tasks, I refer them to a psychiatrist who specialises in mood disorders. When a person is immobilised by their depression, talk therapy has little benefit. Once the medication starts working, talk therapy can be used again.

How can we help ourselves?

I strongly believe in empowering the individual to take responsibility for her own healing process and continued personal growth. Part of my therapy involves teaching the individual to self-manage and take control, so she is no longer a victim of circumstance. Build-ing self-esteem is critical in treating depression, as many people who suffer from depression lose their sense of self.

WHAT GOES AROUND COMES AROUND

WHEN WE DO GOOD DEEDS OR GO OUT OF OUR WAY TO BE THOUGHTFUL TO OTHERS, POSITIVE THINGS HAPPEN.

Research has shown that some factors protect against depression. These include having a close intimate relationship with someone, a full or part-time job away from home and a strong spiritual connection. However, I believe the most powerful antidote to depression is a positive attitude, building a positive self-image and restoring confidence. By trying to stay positive on a continual basis, you can help protect yourself from depression. Monitor any changes in your mood. If you do notice dramatic mood swings, increased stress and anxiety, an increase in alcohol consumption or overeating, try to identify what is happening in your life and get help.

What about those people who simply have a negative attitude?

Some people have a negative disposition caused by feelings of inadequacy and inferiority. This may stem from a negative self-concept, and this mental state is not improved by medication. This is more an attitude problem than a biochemical problem. Psychotherapy can help you improve your self-image and shift negative attitudes.

THIS TOO WILL PASS

THERE ARE GOING TO BE BUMPS IN THE ROAD OF LIFE. WHEN YOU HIT ONE OF THESE BUMPS, REMEMBER, IT WON'T LAST FOREVER. THIS ATTITUDE WILL HELP YOU COPE BETTER DURING DIFFICULT TIMES.

Can you tell us about post-natal depression?

Post-natal depression often takes us by surprise, as it occurs at a time when we expect to be happy and excited about our new baby. The key is to recognise it as early as possible and get it treated. Many mothers experience a few days of the blues after their baby is born. This typically lasts between one and five days and occurs in fifty to eighty per cent of women. During this time, new mothers may be tearful. This is a normal response to the stresses of childbirth. However, if this persists and the mother experiences other symptoms such as inexplicable crying spells, an inability to cope, irritability and feeling totally overwhelmed, then it is possible that she is suffering from post-natal depression.

One of the dangers of severe post-natal depression is that both the mother and the baby are at risk. Someone supportive should be with the mother and baby at all times. With adequate treatment, the depression can be controlled and cured.

What causes post-natal depression?

Post-natal or post-partum depression is the product of altered body chemistry. In many situations it is biochemical in origin and therefore responds well to medication. A general practitioner or a psychiatrist must prescribe medication, and a psychotherapist can provide supportive therapy to assist with the recovery process.

A woman may feel guilty that she is feeling depressed and may feel a sense of failure, believing she is an inadequate mother. Psychotherapy can provide reassurance and relief for distress and despair. Without treatment there is always a danger of suicide and of the depression continuing for a longer time.

Can extreme sadness over the death of a loved one lead to depression?

Yes, depression can be caused by a traumatic event. While normal grief is not an illness and does not require medication, grief can deteriorate into a depression that responds well to medication. We need to learn to distinguish between normal grief and a depression. Some practitioners believe in prescribing medication for normal grief. This can provide temporary relief but it can also dull the reaction and stop a person from experiencing the normal stages of grief, which we will discuss in the next chapter. To numb the mind with medication can be counter-productive. However, if the person does become severely depressed, medication may be necessary.

Can you explain bipolar disorder?

A small percentage of people with depression suffer from bipolar disorder, which used to be known as manic depression. The key feature of bipolar disorder is the tendency of manic episodes to alternate with depressive episodes. In a manic period the individual feels energetic, high, almost euphoric. This is usually followed by a period of deep depression. This may be the result of a change in biochemistry.

Symptoms of the manic phase include an increase in energy, extravagance, and little need for sleep, feelings of omnipotence and impulsive behaviour. The patient may see no reason to seek help or take medication during this phase because she feels on top of the world.

What's the best way to treat bipolar disorder?

Bipolar disorder is difficult to treat, especially in the manic phase, as the patient often denies she has a problem. But the high or manic episodes are often followed by full-blown depression. A maintenance regime of medication is the best treatment.

A psychiatrist who specialises in mood disorders may prescribe the patient lithium or other mood stabilisers to restore her equilibrium. If the patient stops the medication she exposes herself to a relapse. Patients need to have therapy to have the dangers of leaving bipolar disorder untreated explained to them.

What about depression which emerges as a result of a childhood trauma?

Some depressions have their origin in a traumatic event such as childhood abuse. The person may be emotionally scarred and unable to experience normal emotions. In these cases, surface psychotherapy will not be adequate. Deeper intensive therapy, which investigates past events, will be more effective. There are also people who have a genetic predisposition to depression and although there is not always a visible trigger factor, this person is vulnerable. Families may also need to be counselled to assist them in dealing with their depressed family member.

Toolbox

- Learn to recognise the signs of depression.
- Remember that depression may last from a few weeks to a few months.
- If you or someone close to you is experiencing any of the listed symptoms, get help as soon as possible.
- Depression may be treated with a combination of psychotherapy and medication. Only GPs or psychiatrists can prescribe medication.
- If you have had, or are about to have, a baby, alert yourself to the possibility of post-partum depression.
- Bipolar disorder differs from depression in that it is characterised by manic episodes that alternate with down periods.
- Depressions can have their origin in a traumatic life event.
- Using relaxation techniques and medication can relieve anxiety.
- Depression can be hereditary.

chapter three

Surviving Grief and Loss

CYNDI SHARES HER FEELINGS OF when her father died.

I remember clearly how I felt when my father died, even though the event occurred fifteen years ago. He was ill and my brother suggested I return to South Africa to see him. I left on the first available flight. When I arrived he was already in intensive care. We talked. He knew he was going to die. He said he felt satisfied that he had a good life. He was able to say his goodbyes to the family. A few days later he went into a coma and died.

My first feeling was a sense of unreality. I felt numb; I couldn't imagine what the world would feel like without him in it. I felt grateful that we had a very loving relationship and that we had been able to say everything we needed to each other. I know it is painful to live with regrets when someone you love has died and you have unresolved issues.

I needed to be busy and found myself going shopping to buy myself a new dress for the funeral. It seemed important that I wear something pretty for my father as he enjoyed seeing me look beautiful. When I look back now, it seems absurd to have gone shopping the day after my father died, but it felt right at the time.

I coped well while family and friends were around me. It was weeks later that the loss finally hit me. I was out for a walk and suddenly began to sob and sob, as if my heart would break. One of my neighbours drove by, saw me, and took me home. She gave me a cup of strong tea, lots of Kleenex, and allowed me to cry without asking questions. Now that I know a little more about the grief process, I understand my own reactions, and am better able to support someone else dealing with a loss.

There are many times in each of our lives when we will need to deal with loss. We experience loss when someone close to us dies, when a meaningful relationship ends, and even when we move from one stage of our lives to another. We feel loss of youth as we age, loss of our children when they leave home and loss of roots when we move from one place to another. We may also experience the loss of our job, status or position if we are retrenched or retire. If we become ill, we lose our health. In our culture we are very focused on beginnings, from the first words to the first step, the first home, the first job, the first car. We are less able to cope with endings and death.

Elisabeth Kübler-Ross, an expert on death and dying, says in her book *Death – The Final Stage of Growth*, 'Death is as much a part of human existence, of human growth and development, as being born. Death is not an enemy to be conquered. It is an integral part of our life that gives meaning to human existence'. By becoming aware that our lives are finite, we can put more energy into the limited time we have. Kübler-Ross urges us to see death as an invisible yet friendly companion on life's journey. Many years ago I adopted as my personal credo: 'Live every day as if it were your last'. The impact of these words gives my life a sense of urgency and intensity. This belief enables me to achieve many things that I may not have achieved without it.

However, we live in a culture that is uncomfortable with death. We deny its existence. We avoid talking about death with a dying person. We don't know how to grieve or prepare for death. By understanding the grieving process we can learn to cope with loss and different stages of our life.

Grieving and crying are a natural response to loss. These feelings are available to us if we do not suppress them, but from an early age we are taught to suppress our pain, to hide our tears and pretend we are not hurting inside. In this chapter we will explore the grieving process and develop coping skills that will allow us to grow through pain and loss.

Why is death such a taboo subject?

Although death and loss have always been part of life, many of us fear dying – both its mystery and its finality. All of us are going to die, no matter what our status or economic situation, and at some point we are going to lose someone we love. Facing death makes us aware of our vulnerability. It is the uncontrollable aspect of life. We need to accept that death and loss is part of the life process.

What are the first emotions we feel when we experience loss?

Initially, we may feel absolutely numb or anaesthetised. The body often shuts down. Things around us may feel unreal. People around us may think we are coping, but in reality, we haven't yet allowed ourselves to accept the loss or acknowledge the pain.

Having something to do at this stage helps with the process, such as arranging the funeral, writing a eulogy, or advising friends of the death. Many people may refer to this stage as denial, but it is also a protective mechanism of the body to shut out pain while it comes to terms with the loss. As we have said, loss comes in many shapes and forms. The most direct loss we all suffer is that of the death of someone close. What we feel depends on our relationship to the person who has died, on how he died, whether it was sudden, traumatic or expected (after a long illness), and also on our own state of mind at the time of the loss.

The amount of pain we experience relates directly to how attached we are to the person who died. For example, losing a child is devastating. Losing a spouse changes the shape of one's whole day-to-day existence. Losing a parent can be shattering, but it is the natural order of things, and we expect it to happen. If you lose someone in a violent accident or traumatic circumstances, you will have to deal with shock as well as grief.

What are the physical manifestations of grief?

We may experience changes in our sleep patterns, lose our appetite, burst into tears and not be able to control our emotions. Our memory and concentration may also deteriorate. We may also feel lethargic and lack motivation for our usual interests and activity. We may also feel anxious, uncertain and confused.

What is the final stage of the grieving process?

The ultimate goal in the grieving process is acceptance. We need to accept the loss so that we can heal our pain and continue our lives. When we accept our loss we begin to resolve some of the feelings that accompanied it. We may re-evaluate our lives, we may choose to do things differently, and we may discover that new opportunities open up as a result of our loss.

What is the impact of losing a parent?

No-one is ever totally prepared for the feelings that emerge after the death of a parent. We may think we are ready, but when the event occurs, we realise we are not. The grief we feel may be very emotionally draining. If you can, talk to your siblings about the loss of your parent. Each of you is likely to experience the event in a different way, depending on the relationship you had with your parent. If there is some unfinished business with the parent that died, writing a letter describing how you feel can be helpful.

Work towards forgiving your parent for any faults or mistakes. Parents do their best and are sometimes unaware of any pain they cause. If your other parent is still alive make sure you are a support to her. Help her with the practical arrangements for the funeral and with sorting out business or personal affairs. Often the time that precedes the death of a parent is more stressful than the loss itself, especially if the parent had a critical illness. Here is a case study that illustrates the difficulties of living in a different country from a parent who is terminally ill.

SUE, AGED 35, HAD MOVED from Canada to marry an Australian. After two years in Sydney, she was still struggling to create a social circle and make friends. One reason for this was that her husband, Mark, did not have an existing group of friends. He focused on his work and sport, so it was up to Sue to make her own friends. This was difficult for her. Another major issue in her life was that her mother, who still lived in Canada, was ill with a terminal disease.

I went back to see her, but I knew I could not stay indefinitely and look after her. I had to return to Mark. When I got back to Sydney, I felt that Mark wasn't giving me empathy, understanding or support. He was not in touch with his feelings and therefore found it difficult to accept and understand mine. I was grieving for my mother, and was angry with Mark for not providing the support that I needed.

We went to Susie for counselling. She suggested that besides working on the marriage, I should have some sessions with her on my own to work through my feelings of grief. She gave me this option because she felt that Mark, although he had many positive qualities, did not have the capacity to support me in this difficult time. Mark has never been the kind of man who could talk about painful feelings.

I still needed him to understand how much it hurt me that I would soon lose my mother. I felt so torn that I live in Australia and she lives in Canada so I couldn't be by her side in the last painful months of her life. At times I felt frustrated and angry with Mark for not showing me the understanding that I needed. My grief and anger caused us many arguments.

I went to Susie a number of times and shared my pain. This helped me come to terms with the grief. At the same time I continued to have sessions with Mark in which we worked on improving our relationship. I was also investing time in creating friendships. In our joint sessions, Susie explained to Mark how I was feeling and this helped him to be more compassionate and supportive.

How do we feel when we lose a partner?

When your partner dies, it may feel as though your whole world has come apart. You will probably feel numb for a while. Depending on how long you have been together and the intensity of the relationship, you may feel as if you have lost part of yourself. If you have been together for a long time, every aspect of your life will have been intertwined. The world may seem unreal without the familiarity of the person you love. If you are a young widow with young children or if you have lost a mate after many years of marriage, there may be additional issues to deal with, including the added stress of learning to manage the financial affairs, as well as creating a new social life.

Is our grief different when it has been a suicide?

Suicide leaves a painful legacy to survivors. Families of suicide victims often feel guilty, asking themselves if there was something they could have done to prevent the tragedy. Grief counselling may be even more necessary when there has been a suicide.

What can we do to cope with our grief?

Judy Freiman, a specialist bereavement therapist, has some useful advice:

One of the first emotions to surface may be rage or anger. For example, a woman may be angry that her husband has died, leaving her to cope on her own. This anger may be accompanied by guilt or shame. We feel guilty for experiencing anger towards a person who has died. We may feel abandoned by that person. This is often the case with children who lose parents.

'We may then become depressed, tearful and sad. The pain of the loss finally hits us. The worst thing to do to someone in this situation is to say 'Get over it.' People need time to grieve. If they don't go through their feelings of loss and grief at the time of losing someone, those feelings will resurface later on.

Just when everyone expects you to start feeling better and get on with your life, you may fall into a heap. You may feel fragile, vulnerable, slow and unable to concentrate. At this point it is vital to get some outside help. This may include talking to a priest, a professional bereavement therapist or good friends. Try to cut down your work responsibilities if you can afford to.

Allow yourself to mourn, as this is the first step towards healing. In our society, grief is hidden in secrecy. There is a shame associated with being bereft. We are expected to adopt the stiff upper lip and 'get on with it'.

We often don't allow ourselves to grieve until our survival is secure. When a person feels that he is coping with a death, he then starts to experience the pain of the loss. He starts to understand and adjust to an environment where the deceased person is missing.

We may have the same emotions after a relationship breakdown. We have to recreate a physical, social and practical life without the person who was an integral part of it. This happens when our children leave home, when we become ill, or when we move cities or countries.

Allow yourself to cry. Shedding tears is part of the healing process. If you are supporting a friend or relative who has experienced loss, the best thing you can say is, 'I'm with you'. Allow her to cry and be sad if that's how she feels. Don't feel compelled to cheer her up. One of the hardest aspects of bereavement is that grief takes patience. It is not a problem to be "fixed". There is no solution. There is just a journey towards acceptance. When we lose someone close to us, we lose part of ourselves as well. Part of us dies with the person we love, whether it is a parent, a spouse or a child. There are times we may feel we have lost so much of ourselves that we struggle to go on. We may feel depressed and even suicidal.

If you do feel overwhelmed by your feelings of grief and loss, reach out for professional help. Bereavement therapy is very specialised, and having guidance to process your pain will have long-term benefits. Also ask your friends for support. (You may not be able to depend on them entirely, however, if they do not have the patience to see you through your grief.)

Keep a daily journal. Write down your feelings. Write a letter to the person who has died, telling them how you felt about them, what life is like without them, and express any regrets you have about the relationship. One of the most difficult aspects of loss is coming to terms with any unresolved issues you may have had.

It is also vital to take care of yourself physically. Eat well, exercise regularly and don't isolate yourself socially.

What about losing a child?

The death of a child is the most devastating loss that a parent can endure. When a child dies, parents have to confront the incomprehensible reality: 'My child has died before me'.

At the time of the loss, most parents do not know how they will survive. They question how they will be able to continue their lives. Parents always feel responsible for their child; the death brings on enormous guilt because they feel they have failed in some way. They may feel powerless, worthless and inadequate.

Can you share some of your experiences of grief and loss when you worked at the hospital?

When I worked at the children's hospital, we sometimes came across parents who had lost a child in a car accident. I would take the parents into casualty and encourage them to sit down with their child for as long as they wanted or needed. I offered to be with them but suggested they had some time alone with their child. This would give them an opportunity to talk to their child about anything that came into their minds. This might include reminiscing or expressing their tremendous grief. It would also enable them to say goodbye. I feel this is an important first step of the grieving process that should be available to all parents when they lose a child, close relative or friend. Hospitals nowadays are more in touch with the needs of parents. They offer ongoing grief counselling or refer the bereaved to specialist therapists.

How does a parent ever come to terms with such a loss?
Patience is essential. You have to take as much time as you need. Everyone heals in different ways. The rate of healing depends on three things: the parent's relationship with the child, the parent's emotional and mental state, and the support system of relatives, friends and others.

Parents struggling to come to terms with their loss will often need a friend, therapist or spiritual advisor to guide them through their pain. Although parents will find ways to survive losing their child, many never get over the loss.

What is the impact of losing a child on a couple's relationship?
The impact can be devastating. Parents may experience the loss of a child early on, when a baby is stillborn or dies shortly after birth. When they lose a baby, they lose their hopes, dreams and expectations even though they did not have the opportunity to get to know their baby. When a child dies suddenly through an accident or acute illness, the parents may be left feeling shocked as well as devastated. Parents suffer desperately no matter what the age of the child.

Partners may express their grief in different ways. Often the male is unable to express his emotions openly, which may lead to his partner misunderstanding how he feels. He may feel pressure to be strong and take care of his wife. He has no-one to support him in his grief.

One partner may talk incessantly to everyone about the loss. The other may withdraw and shut down completely. One partner may bury himself in his work as a means of escaping the pain. The other partner may resort to alcohol, medication or overeating in order to find solace.

One case I worked on involved a car accident where both parents died, leaving three boys under the age of thirteen. A battle ensued between family members for custody of the boys. It made me realise how important it is for parents to nominate a guardian for each child in their will, as soon as each child is born. They should choose carefully – a person who has similar values to their own. The guardian also needs to be aware of his responsibilities in the event of a tragedy.

Parents may have an urgent need to discover why the child died. This attempt to lay blame may alienate the other spouse and cause a breakdown of trust. It is not unusual for couples to separate after losing a child. The pain of the loss is a trauma that puts tremendous strain on the relationship.

If a couple is struggling to support each other in their grief, they may find it reassuring to join a group or have couples therapy.

Could you talk about other forms of loss?

When a relationship ends, be it a love affair, a marriage or a friendship, we experience loss, and we may well go through similar stages to bereavement grief. (In chapters 11 and 12 we look at what happens when a relationship ends.)

Another strong emotion of loss occurs as we age. We mourn youth, health and unfulfilled dreams. Our body changes, and we may have less energy. We may mourn our unfulfilled dreams and unhappy relationships. It is therefore vital to be pro-active in terms of accomplishing your goals and experiencing happy, harmonious relationships.

When we become ill, we also feel a sense of loss. Financial difficulties, job loss, emigration, moving house and children leaving home may all produce similar emotions.

The key to coping with these feelings is to not suppress them or push them away. Feeling sad, and experiencing a sense of loss and emptiness, is part of life. At other times we feel joy, excitement and happiness. Allow yourself to feel the pain and hurt, but if you find yourself sinking low, not able to sleep, eat, concentrate or connect with friends, accept that you may need help.

You mentioned the experience of losing a home, relocation or emigration. Many of us have moved house, town or country and struggled to come to terms with a feeling of loss. Is this a kind of grieving as well?

When we move homes, we need to allow ourselves to go through the complete grieving process. It is vital to say a proper goodbye to your old home and your possessions if they mean a lot to you. You may even find it liberating to give away possessions to friends or relatives who may need them. In doing this you create space for the new. Before relocating to your new country or town, visit the places that are special to you and think about why they mean so much to you.

YOU CAN'T ALWAYS CHOOSE WHAT HAPPENS TO YOU, BUT YOU CAN ALWAYS CHOOSE YOUR RESPONSE

HAVING THAT CHOICE EMPOWERS YOU.

When I left my home town at thirty, I spent nine months saying a lingering goodbye to all my favourite places, and by the time I was ready to leave I felt I carried all the love inside me in the form of special memories. When I reached my destination, Sydney, I was ready to explore, discover and connect with the new. I agree that proper goodbyes can help with letting go and moving forward.

The same goes for age. At each stage of our life we enjoy different experiences and then there may come a time to move on. One of these critical phases is when our children leave home. For a woman, this time often coincides with menopause, so at a time of vulnerability, she is also dealing with a major life change.

CYNDI SHARES HER FEELINGS AT the time of her mastectomy to illustrate another example of loss.

I recently underwent a mastectomy, so I had to grieve the loss of a breast. I can pinpoint two distinct phases. The first was the crisis. I had to come to terms with the shock of having a mastectomy, surgery, cancer and all that it entailed. I'm very good with crises. I don't panic, I keep calm, and I focus on the big picture. For me this meant seeing the loss in perspective. I realised that I had my health and my life. Losing a breast was a small price to pay.

Initially I felt very positive and thought I had put the experience behind me. Just when I thought I was over it, I felt a tremendous surge of tears, pain and grief. I understand now that I only grieved when I felt safe to express my feelings. Every day when I dress and undress, I am confronted with a big space on my chest and I feel a mixture of shock and surprise. I have to learn to accept my body, which has changed forever.

I remember being invited to a wedding and realising that not one of my evening dresses would be suitable now that I had only one breast. I went shopping. All the dresses I tried on were strapless or off the shoulder. None of them would fit, as with my prosthesis, I required a conventional bra to hold it. I became very despondent. It was the day before the wedding and I had nothing to wear. A thoughtful friend came to my rescue. She drove me to the city and took me to a boutique where I found the perfect outfit, a long skirt and knit top. It was a flattering style, and there was no risk of revealing straps or low necklines.

Once I had found a solution, I felt better. I know that the grieving is not over. However, on most days I spend no more than a few minutes thinking about my missing breast. My life is full, my days are busy, and I am blessed to be well and free of cancer. It is life that counts, not the missing breast. The experience has given me a greater compassion and empathy for others who have to cope with more serious disabilities on a daily basis. So I am learning to cope as I go along.

What do you recommend to best cope with this sort of loss?
Once again, allow yourself to go through the grieving process. Feel the sadness, allow the tears to flow. Once you have experienced the pain of the loss, you will feel more ready to move on. Plan new activities. Enrich your life by learning, connecting with people and finding outlets for your energies.

When life is disrupted by loss, we can either ignore our feelings and suppress the emotions, or we can connect with our feelings and move beyond the pain. The loss we each experience will vary in intensity. By understanding the process, we give ourselves the opportunity of growing through loss. Change is inevitable, so learning to grieve and move on is an essential life tool.

This extract is one of my favourite writings on the subject of grief. Mitch Albom, author of *Tuesdays with Morrie*, wrote, 'Learn how to live and you'll know how to die. Learn how to die, and you'll know how to live'. This message is for those with terminal illness as well as for the healthy. Open yourself up to life, connect with people in a meaningful way, and develop a spiritual connection. This can be a way of tapping into your inner strength.

Toolbox

- Give yourself time to grieve. Don't rush the process.
- Be patient: allow yourself to feel the pain before you heal.
- Crying calms you and acts as a natural tranquilliser.
- Develop a support system for help in times of trouble.
- Rituals can help with the grieving process. Involve family and friends in the process.
- If you feel overwhelmed by your feelings of loss, go to a bereavement therapist.
- Strengthen your spiritual connections. This does not have to involve participation in formal religion. It can include prayer, meditation and community.
- Write a letter to the person who is no longer with you. Allow yourself to say the things you wish you had said when that person was alive.
- Get as much help as you need, when you need it.
- Try to give yourself some time off work so that you can focus on your feelings. You may also find it difficult to concentrate on your work.

chapter four

Understanding and Managing Stress

CAROLE IS A FORTY-YEAR-OLD MOTHER with two teenage children. She recently married for the second time, after having been a single mum for some time. Although the family seemed to be settling in well together, a few weeks into the new marriage Carole felt emotionally drained and exhausted. When she could cope no longer, she came to see me.

It seemed incongruous that I should be feeling bad when things were going so well. But after a few sessions with Susie, I discovered the source of my problem. As a single mother, I had given a great deal of time and energy to my children. I wanted to be there for them. Then when I married, I wanted to give time and attention to my new husband. My work as a full-time practitioner was very demanding. I felt overwhelmed.

After a long day's work with life-threatening emergencies, I would come home and go straight into the kitchen to prepare dinner. After we had eaten, my children would go to their rooms to study. My husband would go to the lounge room to read or watch television. I would go back into the kitchen and bake cakes and cook elaborate dishes for my family and friends.

Susie asked me if my family was demanding. I said that they weren't, I simply wanted to do all of this for them. She asked me why;

what need was I trying to satisfy? I realised my primary need was to be a perfect wife and mother. I wanted to please everyone. Finally we realised the reason I spent so much time in the kitchen was because it was neutral territory. I was equally accessible to both my husband and of my children, and was doing something equally for all of them. There was no reason for anyone to feel jealous.

I realised I could not keep up the pace. Once I was aware of what I was doing, I could let myself off the hook.

We all experience stress in our day-to-day life. It is an inevitable and inescapable aspect of living. However, there are two kinds of stress. The first is positive, energising and motivating. It is a force that gets us moving and galvanises us into action. The other type of stress has a negative effect on us. This is when we experience an overload of stress from a situation, producing fatigue, exhaustion, physical illness or tension.

We all have a different threshold of stress tolerance. Some of us can stay calm in stressful situations, others react strongly. Indeed, some people appear to thrive on stress, while others may feel more stressed, even with a lighter workload.

You need to learn to identify which situations you find difficult so that you can better manage the stress in your life. Some of us may use an enormous amount of emotional energy worrying about things that may never happen. We may also overreact to incidents that are insignificant in the big picture. Understand your emotional threshold and examine your response to stressful situations.

When we refer to someone as being stressed, we perceive that she has too many demands placed on her. Some of these may be under her control, others she has to accept and find a way of coping with. All of the issues below may increase the level of stress in a person's life. They are also the common reasons that people give for feeling stressed:

- Relationship is in trouble.
- Financial pressures.
- Family demands.
- Ill health or chronic pain.
- Deadlines or work overload.
- Too many tasks to do in too little time.
- Feeling out of control.
- Feeling insecure about future plans.
- Not enough personal time.
- Frustration at work.
- Boredom, monotony or lack of stimulation.

What are the symptoms of stress?

People react to stress in different ways. They may become irritable and short-tempered, tired and yet unable to sleep. Their behaviour differs from the norm.

Some may turn to alcohol, drugs, food or smoking for relief. Others may experience a physical illness, body tension, fatigue, anger, depression or symptoms such as nausea, headaches, backache, or even resort to violence. Clearly stress needs to be understood and managed.

What can we do to manage stress in our life?

First of all, for something to be stressful, we have to perceive it as a cause for stress. Sometimes we exaggerate a situation's potential effect so that it becomes stressful.

Secondly, we often undermine our ability to manage problems. By expecting a situation to be difficult, we perceive it as stressful. If you don't expect to cope, you probably won't. Your expectations determine the outcome, so you can increase your stress level by imagining a negative outcome. Conversely, with positive expectations, you have the power to diminish the level of stress. So choosing your attitude can be the key to the amount of stress you suffer.

How can we avoid excessive stress in our lives?

If you can identify the causes of stress in your life, you can then learn to deal with stress in a constructive way:

- Plan your time, and write down everything that you have to do each day.
- Make sure you have enough time for yourself each week, for the things you enjoy doing.
- Spend time with friends – social contact is therapeutic.
- Exercise regularly.
- Make sure you have something to look forward to – holidays and treats.

How can you shift from negative to positive expectations of a situation?

You can draw from your own experience. If you have handled a similar problem before, you can remind yourself that you are confident of tackling the problem. You can actually train yourself to think more realistically. Do a quick 'reality' check. How realistic are your fears? If you are in the habit of expecting negative outcomes, you can use positive self-talk to shift the direction of your thinking. Ask yourself, 'What is the worst thing that can happen?'

You used that technique with me before I had my hysterectomy, when I was feeling very anxious. One day you said to me, 'Get real, what are you anxious about?' I explained that I was worried that I would not get better after surgery. You made me realise how unrealistic this line of thinking was. From then on, I did a reality check and the anxiety disappeared.

I'm glad I was able to help you with that situation. Often we need to 'reframe' problems so that we can change our attitude towards dealing with them.

Another cause of stress is feeling that we are not in control of things. How can we cope with this feeling?
We only feel out of control if there are too many demands being placed on us. One of the effective ways of looking at this problem is to examine your time management skills. Do you have a plan of action that you follow or do you respond to problems as they arise?

I make lists of all the tasks I have to do, writing them in order of priority. I use a diary, and taking a week at a time, I work out when I can tackle each task. I do the difficult tasks first. Once they are out of the way, I feel energised enough to tackle the others. Getting things done gives you a sense of accomplishment and helps you feel in control. Have a weekly plan and a daily action list. Don't procrastinate, as the stress of not doing something important increases as you put it off.

You did this for me when we were writing this book. I must confess I am nowhere near as organised as you are! You forced me to be on track and finish the book on time.

If you have a problem, break it down into small components that make it easier to manage. If you feel overwhelmed by work commitments, sit down with a paper and pen, and break down the problem into its component parts. Work out a plan to tackle the problem step by step.

What is the best way to cope with uncertainty? We all have a certain amount of it in our lives, but it can be very stressful.
We all have the capacity to live with some uncertainty, as life is full of the unexpected. But we also need security to give our lives predictability and comfort. Look at the sources of insecurity in your life and see what you can do to remove the stress. Perhaps you feel insecure about the progress of a relationship, your job, where you intend to live or even where you go on holiday. Set

yourself a date by which a decision needs to be made. Be prepared to go out on a limb and take some risks to reach an outcome.

JOHN, AGED FORTY-FIVE, CAME TO see me as he was feeling very stressed. He was a successful businessman, but worked long hours and felt that he never had any time for himself. He wasn't enjoying his life.

I'm a perfectionist. I find it very hard to delegate in my business, yet I can't do it all myself. I travel extensively, and deadlines, traffic and commitments dominate my days. I find my life very stressful.

Susie encouraged me to make some changes. We drew up a list of functions in my business that I could hand over to other people. Susie suggested I look at my perfectionism as something that could be creating a great deal of stress, not just for me but also for others in my work environment as well as my family. I had to learn to let go of my desire to do everything perfectly.

We looked at my weekly schedule and Susie asked me to block out some time each week for relaxation or recreation. This included a game of tennis, time with my partner and children, as well as twenty minutes of meditation each day. At first I thought I could never find the time to slot these activities into an already heavy schedule. However, it was amazing that with careful planning, not only did I manage to find the time, but I was much more relaxed at the end of the day. To cope with my schedule, Susie suggested I get to appointments, airports and meetings at least ten minutes earlier than scheduled. This reduced the stress and gave me time to relax. She also encouraged me to plan each week ahead and to say 'no' to commitments that were not a priority.

Over a short period of time I began feeling more relaxed, my business operated more efficiently and my family was happier, as I spent more time with them, and I definitely started to enjoy life more.

What can we do if we feel exhausted or burnt out?

You must ask yourself if you are taking on too much. What can you let go? Is there any way you can simplify your life? Do you have enough recreation and relaxation in your life? It can be difficult to have time for relaxation every day but if you take a break each week from your work and routine commitments, you will feel refreshed and invigorated. If you feel overwhelmed by work demands, you may have to discuss this with your boss and set some workload limits.

If you ignore the warning signs and allow the stress to increase, you may overdo it and experience severe physical and emotional symptoms such as frequent illness or even a nervous breakdown. When you notice negative feelings such as anxiety, anger or fear, try to identify the specific cause. Once you pinpoint the source of stress, you can act on it. Examine how you think about an event. Can you change your response? Get in touch with your feelings. We often don't allow ourselves to experience pain, sadness or anger, suppressing those emotions as they cause us stress. Let these feelings out.

Is there anything else we can do to make our lives less stressful?

Physical exercise is very effective at reducing the symptoms of stress. Find something you enjoy that you can do on a regular basis, such as tennis, walking, dancing, swimming, or aerobics.

What about crying?

Having a good cry can also make you feel better. Allowing yourself to weep now and again will produce an internal chemical reaction that will improve your mood.

Sometimes when we are very stressed, we have sleeping problems and we wake up tired. What can we do about this?

Insomnia can be a result of stress, but lack of sleep causes more stress, so it is vital to tackle the problem early on. One of the things that may help you overcome insomnia is the use of relaxation tapes. I have made a relaxation tape that I give to my clients who have difficulty falling asleep. They all tell me that they are asleep before the tape finishes. It basically guides you through a process of gradual mental and physical relaxation. You tense and then let go each part of the body until you have released tension. This enables you to take the focus away from the thoughts that are troubling you. There are many different kinds of relaxation tapes available now, which you can obtain from bookshops, by mail order and from the Internet.

Another helpful hint is to establish a going to bed ritual. This may include a hot shower, some warm milk and some reading light reading. Don't take files of work to bed. Try not to do anything mentally stimulating just before bedtime. Establish a regular bedtime pattern and a similar waking time.

We seem to feel unsettled if we have too little sleep or if we have too much. Broken sleep makes us feel cranky and irritable. Resorting to sleeping tablets creates dependency and does not establish healthy sleeping habits. Avoid coffee or caffeine-based drinks in the evening.

Try this exercise. Take twenty very deep breaths. When you breathe out, say to yourself, 'Relax'. Tell yourself, 'I am falling asleep. I will sleep peacefully and wake at 7 am'. Your mind cannot focus on positive and negative at the same time. Choose to think realistic, positive thoughts.

What about if you have no trouble falling asleep but you wake at 2 am and are unable to go back to sleep?

This often happens when we are feeling anxious. We are exhausted so we fall asleep easily but then wake and are plagued by worrying thoughts. If this happens, don't try to force yourself to sleep. Get up, make yourself a warm drink, and try using a relaxation tape, or read until you feel drowsy.

Another technique, which may help, is to have a pad and pen next to you so that you can write down any worrying thoughts as they come to you. They then lose their power to keep you awake. In the middle of the night things often feel more serious than they really are, so write it all down and identify what you are worrying about. The more you lie awake and worry, the less likely you are to fall asleep. Use positive self-talk, and reassure yourself that you will cope with the problem.

Is it wise to take sleeping pills?

Sleeping pills are still the most common form of treatment used for insomnia. You would have to consult a doctor to get a prescription. However, drugs will not treat the cause of the problem nor will they enable you to establish a healthy sleep pattern. When you stop taking the pills, you will go back to restless sleep. There may be some acute situations where sleeping medication is the best approach but it is not a long-term solution for stress, anxiety, depression or insomnia.

'I AM AN OLD MAN, I HAVE HAD MANY WORRIES. MOST OF THEM DID NOT HAPPEN'

MANY OF US WASTE ENERGY WORRYING ABOUT THINGS THAT NEVER HAPPEN. THIS ENERGY COULD BE USED MUCH MORE PRODUCTIVELY. MY MOTHER TENDS TO BE A WORRIER, AND I SAY TO HER, 'MUM, KEEP YOUR EYES ON THE DOUGHNUT AND NOT ON THE HOLE.'

How can we establish better sleep patterns?

Write a journal for one week. Record the time you went to bed, the time you woke up, how many hours you slept for and how you felt when you woke up. This may help you identify some of the causes of your sleep problems. Then make a contract with yourself. Set a regular time to go to bed, decide how many hours you would like to sleep and make sure you do some relaxation before you drift off to sleep.

What else makes us feel stressed?

We will become stressed when we deny our own feelings and needs. It is often difficult to accept that we have negative feelings. We may feel guilty if we feel angry, hurt, jealous, bitter or frightened. We may not know how to cope with these feelings, and deny or suppress them. These feelings are usually experienced somatically, such as nausea, tummy aches, tension in the neck or back, dry mouth, loss of appetite or headaches.

So what can we do when these bad feelings come up for us?

When you become aware of a negative feeling, stop and notice where you are experiencing the feeling in your body. Identify what is making you feel bad. Ask yourself, 'Is there something constructive I can do to change or improve the situation?' 'Am I overreacting?' 'What is the worst thing that can happen?'

Then say to yourself, 'I can deal with this'. Create an action plan, including a few simple things you can do to improve how you feel about the situation. What is important is not what happens to us in life, but how we handle it. You are entitled to have 'bad' feelings. But you can also choose how you will deal with them.

I know exactly what you mean. When I first received my diagnosis of breast cancer, I had a choice between panic and anticipating the worst, or focusing on a positive outcome. As I am well, I am glad I did not invest all my emotional energy into panic, worry and imagining worst-case scenarios. Being positive about the situation could well have played a big part in my recovery.

The mind is a very powerful tool. We can teach ourselves to think positively, assess the situation and expect to cope. This influences how we tackle a problem. The more we do this, the more this pattern of thinking becomes part of us.

What happens when we deny our own needs?

Often we may act like a martyr, denying our needs – relaxation time, connecting with friends or just unwinding. But we are not robots; if we ignore our needs we will become tense, irritable, resentful and unable to function well.

We may feel that time and money spent on ourselves is a luxury and that we should sacrifice our own needs to meet the needs of others. But we owe it to those we love to look after ourselves and give our own needs equal priority. If we don't, we become more difficult to live with. This can put further stress on our relationships.

Make a list of ten activities that you enjoy. Then reward yourself every week by doing at least three of them. This could include listening to music, going for a swim, reading a novel or having lunch with a friend. Schedule in these activities no matter how busy you think will be. Relaxation time will refresh you.

The inability to make decisions can cause us stress. How can we overcome this problem?

Yes, another source of stress is the inability to make decisions. Often it is not that important whether you choose A or B. When we are in a situation where we have to choose between two alternatives, it creates a conflict within us. Once you make a choice, you release yourself from the tension and stress of worrying what to do. Allow yourself to make mistakes and be imperfect. Anxiety, worry and indecision cause more stress than most courses of action we choose.

Toolbox

- Don't deny your own needs.
- Get in touch with your feelings.
- Make sure you have sufficient time for relaxation and recreation.
- Make time for regular physical exercise – this should be a priority.
- Cultivate good time-management skills.
- Plan your days to avoid stress. Write down your plan.
- Crying may release stress, so don't hold back your tears.
- Procrastination creates stress. Be more decisive.
- Train yourself to think realistically. Worrying uses up energy and makes you feel anxious.
- If you have trouble sleeping, try relaxation and meditation techniques.

chapter five

Enhancing Communication Skills

JAN AND MICHAEL, BOTH IN their late thirties, came to see me because of problems in their relationship. They were both intelligent people with responsible jobs, yet they complained about their lack of effective communication.

No matter what they discussed, they could not talk to each other in a rational way. Jan felt Michael did not listen to what she had to say. She would walk away and become increasingly withdrawn from Michael as a result of their arguments, or she would end up in tears, with Michael shouting 'There you go again. I can't talk to you without you crying!'

I pointed out that it was acceptable to disagree, but to resolve their arguments, it was necessary to set out some rules that they would both find helpful.

- First, choose a time when you will not be interrupted for at least one hour.
- Tell your partner clearly and calmly how you feel. State what the problem is for you.
- Listen to what the problem is for your partner.
- Attack the problem, not the person.
- Look for answers that will be acceptable to both of you.

- Take turns in speaking. If necessary, set a timer for ten minutes, during which time the other is not to interrupt.
- Avoid being critical.
- Give in if the issue is not important to you, but is important to your partner. Avoid name-calling, put-downs, blaming, threatening, bringing up the past or issues that are not relevant to the subject under discussion.
- Don't be aggressive.
- Deal with one issue at a time.
- Let the other person know you have heard them. Validate their feelings. 'I understand what you are feeling/ saying' doesn't necessarily mean you agree with them but it does make clear that you have appreciated what they are saying.
- Fight fair – don't bring other people or issues into the argument.
- Never go to sleep angry.

TREAT OTHERS THE WAY YOU WOULD WANT THEM TO TREAT YOU

EVEN WHEN YOU ARE ANGRY, BE RESPECTFUL TO THE PERSON WITH WHOM YOU ARE ANGRY. IT IS NOT WHAT YOU SAY, BUT HOW YOU SAY IT. THINK BEFORE YOU SPEAK. WHEN YOU ACT WITH INTEGRITY, YOU GAIN SELF-RESPECT, AS WELL AS RESPECT FROM OTHERS.

We are social beings, interacting with other people every day. We need relationships in order to lead a full and balanced life. The way we connect with people determines the quality of our relationships. When we experience problems in our communication with others, we may feel stressed, lonely or unhappy. Many of us do not have effective communication skills and this may create problems, especially when we need to share negative or bad feelings. The ability to communicate well will help us to create lasting friendships, have healthy family interactions and get things done in our day-to-day life.

In this chapter, we examine three major communication styles and some of the stumbling blocks to effective communication. We also look at loneliness and the best way to overcome it. Learning listening and conflict resolution skills can improve the quality of our relationships. If we communicate clearly, openly and honestly, we encounter less resistance, misunderstandings and negativity from others.

What are the blocks to effective communication?

Communication is a two-way process. One person sends a message and the other receives it. It sounds straightforward enough but information can be misinterpreted simply by a person not listening carefully to the speaker. The emotional state of a person may also prevent him from hearing what is said, or a person may receive conflicting messages.

If a person feels attacked, he will want to attack back or withdraw. The fault could lie with the person who is giving the message or with the one receiving it. Listening is as important as speaking. If you perceive the person you are talking to as stubborn, unreasonable or illogical, you may give up trying to communicate with him as you meet with so much resistance. I often encounter this with parents and teenagers as well as couples in therapy. Learning to give and receive clear messages is a vital skill.

What are the three different styles of communicating?

The ideal way to communicate is assertively, where thoughts, feelings and beliefs are expressed in a direct, honest and appropriate way. You make reasonable requests of others and feel comfortable refusing unacceptable requests made of you. You say what you mean and you mean what you say. We all know where we stand with an assertive person. There are no double meanings. An assertive person uses the language, 'I feel unhappy when ...'

The second form of communicating is the aggressive style. An aggressive person tries to scare others into doing what he wants. Sometimes it works, and this encourages and motivates the aggressive person into continuing his behaviour. He may shout, criticise or display anger. Most aggressive people are acting out of fear caused by low self-esteem and lack of self-confidence. So they bully others to compensate for their own perceived inadequacies.

In some cases, people who have grown up in an abusive family compensate by going to the other extreme, becoming submissive. It is therefore important to learn effective communication skills.

Communicating aggressively will have a negative impact on relationships. A person may feel that to win, he has to threaten, frustrate, humiliate or undermine the other person. This treatment will lose the aggressor respect and trust, and he will find himself isolated, lonely and afraid. If you behave aggressively sometimes, think about the feelings you have at the time. Is there another way you could handle those feelings?

TONY, AGED THIRTY-FIVE, HAD BEEN married to Geraldine for three and a half years. He came to me with a specific problem that he wanted to solve. He felt it would be helpful to discuss his issues with someone neutral.

When I married Geraldine, I didn't realise that I was marrying into her family as well. Geraldine is very close to her family. When conflicts erupted with her family, she felt like the ham in the sandwich. Because her marriage came first, she wanted to resolve issues in a way that would be acceptable to me and would also reunite the family.

Geraldine's sister was extremely jealous of her. She also behaved very badly towards me. One night at the dinner table in our home, she accused me of being racist. I asked her if she would stop her accusations. When she persisted I became angry and asked her to leave my house. I did this in front of everyone. As a result of this interlude she refused to speak to me, which was very upsetting.

Susie suggested a few ideas that might help me handle similar interactions in the future. For example, saying quietly, 'That's very hurtful. I think it is time to end the conversation.' If she persisted, I could choose not to pursue the discussion. In a few sessions, Susie gave me tools to handle difficult family encounters. If situations now arise, I feel I can handle them more effectively before they get out of control. I am less likely to lose my temper or say something I will regret later.

WE ARE TREATED THE WAY WE ALLOW OTHERS TO TREAT US

LET PEOPLE KNOW THAT YOU WANT TO BE TREATED WITH CONSIDERATION AND RESPECT THE VERY FIRST TIME THEIR BEHAVIOUR IS UNACCEPTABLE. AND TREAT YOURSELF WITH RESPECT – TEACH OTHERS HOW YOU WANT TO BE TREATED. THEY WILL FOLLOW YOUR EXAMPLE.

At first I was reluctant to have therapy. I feared that I would be locked in for months on end. Then I agreed to go to a few sessions where we could address some specific problems. Susie brought blocked feelings to the surface and once I had the awareness, she provided me with some different ways to overcome them. It helped to be talking to someone neutral. Susie didn't take sides. If something else comes up in my life, I will go back for a few more sessions. Now that I have a relationship with a therapist, I feel more open to getting help. Susie showed me how to resolve issues without forcing either person to apologise. I have learnt to speak my truth and be honest. I have also learnt to be less aggressive and more diplomatic. Once I had dealt with family issues the friendship with my wife returned. Our communication skills improved and I no longer walked around feeling guilt or pressure.

Tony was able to make some significant changes in a short time. He is aware that it is easy to slip back into old patterns and I encouraged him to return if other issues cropped up. There is usually no quick fix to making lasting changes in oneself or in a relationship. However, if you have a specific problem in your life, four to six sessions, regularly spaced out, can help you deal with those issues.

The third form of communication is the submissive style. These communicators are afraid to assert themselves and stick up for their rights because they are afraid of rejection. When we behave submissively we often end up feeling resentful towards others, and we may also feel angry with ourselves for not being more assertive.

Some people confuse submission with politeness, fearing disapproval from others. If you are a people-pleaser, always doing things for others, then you may need to learn how to say 'no' when something is inconvenient for you. For example, 'I would really like to help you but I have other commitments right now'.

Are women more likely to communicate in a submissive manner?

Yes, women often tend to communicate in a more submissive way, as this behaviour has been handed down from generation to generation. In order to break the cycle, women need to become aware of this pattern of communication. It is also a cultural phenomenon. In our society men are more likely to be aggressive, and women submissive. Both forms of communication are likely to have a negative effect on relationships.

What are the consequences of being a submissive communicator?

Submission may be an easy way out in the short term but in the long term it creates problems in relationships. If you act like a doormat, eventually your partner will treat you with disrespect. You then feel resentful towards that person. In order to be a doormat, you have to lie down and allow someone to walk over you. You have to ask yourself, 'Am I lying down?'

In therapy we often role-play an assertive response. It may feel strange at the beginning but it becomes easier. You will see an improvement in your relationship and you will enjoy the company of others more.

Why is it so important to communicate honestly?

When we communicate, we can either be open and honest with others, or hide our true feelings. If we are not open, others have to guess or mind-read our feelings, and this may result in misunderstandings. Your body language and facial expression may also be giving the wrong impression. There are occasional times, in social and professional circles, where it is necessary to mask our true feelings, but in close relationships we must aim for openness and authenticity.

What about the ability to listen?

Active listening means we really hear what the other person is saying. Often in conversation we are so busy formulating an answer that we miss most of what the other person is saying. This often happens during arguments or heated discussions. We interrupt mid-sentence, either because we anticipate what a person is going to say or we are afraid we may forget what we want to say.

Once we are aware of the obstacles to listening well, we can practise listening actively. Clear your mind of thoughts. Pretend you are a tape recorder, absorbing everything the person is saying. The greatest compliment you can give someone when she is speaking is your full attention. Once she has finished talking, briefly reflect back her message aloud in your own words to show you have been listening. This indicates that you have heard and understood her words. You may not agree with what the person has said, but once you have acknowledged that you have heard them, you can give your point of view.

What are the factors which contribute to shyness?

Most people feel shy in certain social situations, even those who appear to be super-confident. For example, going to a cocktail party or business function at which you don't know anyone can be very nerve-racking. If you find your shyness at all restrictive, you may be afraid of rejection, lack confidence or have low self-esteem, making it difficult for you to make new friends. Shy people may often feel unable to express themselves adequately, feeling self-conscious and inhibited in many situations that require conversation or speaking. This nervousness may prevent them from being able to communic-ate effectively. If you do suffer from debilitating shyness, consider seeing a therapist, who will be able to help you gain confidence.

It might be helpful to think about why you are shy. I remember when I first came to Sydney from Hungary at the age of ten, I couldn't speak English. I didn't know anyone at school and I felt extremely self-conscious. I felt as if I was the only one in the whole school who had no friends. It was many years before I felt I had overcome these early difficulties. It is possible to overcome our shyness. It takes time but it is well worth the effort.

TAKE RESPONSIBILITY FOR YOUR ACTIONS. IT WILL EMPOWER YOU

IF YOU OFTEN SAY, 'IT'S NOT MY FAULT', YOU LEAVE YOURSELF POWERLESS TO MAKE CHANGES. STOP MAKING EXCUSES. TAKE RESPONSIBILITY FOR A SITUATION, AND YOU WILL SEE WHERE YOU WENT WRONG AND HOW YOU CAN DO IT DIFFERENTLY NEXT TIME.

Having one or more friendships can enrich your life, so take some constructive steps to achieve this goal. Plan some activities that open up opportunities to meet other people in non-threatening situations. Take up a hobby, join a sporting club, enroll in an adult education course or learn a craft. Any of these will enable you to meet people with similar interests. It is easier to talk to people if you have something in common or when you are all involved in a mutual task. You can talk about the activity that you are participating in. If you see someone with a friendly face or a person who is also on their own, go up to them and start talking. They will be so grateful to you. Resist the urge to look away and make sure you look the person in the eye and smile .If she seems friendly, you might want to suggest a cup of coffee after the course.

While chatting to your new acquaintance show an interest in her by asking about her job, her family and her interests. Don't divulge too much personal information of your own until you have developed the relationship a little. Opening up too much too soon can leave you vulnerable and embarrassed next time you meet.

By following some of these suggestions you will gradually be able to make friends and connect with others.

Susie, what do you think is the best way to make new friends?

Good friendship provides us with pleasure, laughter, companionship and support. If you find it a struggle to make and sustain friendships, examine your style of communication. Are you submissive or aggressive in the way you interact with others? If your problem is shyness or if you have moved to a new town where you don't know many people, you may need to be creative in establishing ways to make friends. If a new neighbour moves into your street, take the initiative and knock on the door and introduce yourself. Take a cake and make them feel welcome. Or join a club and take up a sport such as tennis or a game like bridge. This will help you meet people with similar interests. Or you could join an adult education class; learn a craft, a new language or even belly dancing! In any group you are bound to discover some like-minded people. Once you find someone you like, suggest doing something together, like going to the movies or out for a coffee or a drink.

What are some other techniques for breaking the ice?

If you feel shy and lost for words, ask the other person about himself. Most people enjoy someone taking an interest in who they are, where they come from and what they think. This will then lead to a conversation in which you share information about yourself. It you feel insecure about having a social conversation, read the paper and keep up with current trends, politics and current affairs. Don't be self-centred. Ask others for their opinion.

Once we've made the initial approach, how should we cultivate a friendship?

It is important to allow trust to develop naturally before you disclose personal and confidential information. I met one of my dearest friends a few years ago at a hands-on cooking class. We started playing bridge, tennis, and going out socially. But we allowed our friendship to develop slowly. Often people who feel a desperate need to make friends may divulge too much too soon. This can lead to them feeling vulnerable and may frighten the new acquaintance off.

Many of us, fearing rejection, do not initiate contact with people. We are sensitive and feel that if someone refuses to connect we are not worthy of friendship. We need to understand that not everyone can be a friend but by exploring a number of connections, we open ourselves up to more potential friendships.

Communication is so important in every facet of your life – in all aspects of your relationship with your family, friends and work. By improving your communications skills, people will respond to you more positively, thereby helping you to gain confidence to be more open to future friendships.

Toolbox

- Understand your own patterns of communication.
- Ask yourself if these patterns are serving your relationships.
- Do you need to make any changes?
- Practise assertive behaviour.
- Listen attentively when others speak to you.
- Learn to enjoy your own company.
- Smile at people.
- Nurture new friendships and family connections.
- If you are lonely, explore some courses or activities you might enjoy.

chapter six

Managing Anger

JEFF MARRIED CATHY AFTER KNOWING her for less than a year.

I was 22. We were both on the rebound from failed relationships. I suddenly found myself married and in a high-stress job. Shortly after our wedding, Cathy fell pregnant.

We had serious problems from the start. I was immature. I hadn't travelled or tasted freedom. I was working seven days a week and Cathy felt abandoned, coping with the baby alone. We bickered constantly. We would yell at each other, throw things, and our sexual relationship disintegrated. I had a bad temper and found it difficult to control my anger.

When our baby was eight months old, Cathy moved out. Then we got back together for a trial period and she got pregnant again. We had not discussed having another baby and once more I felt trapped and angry. I hated going home at night. We slept in separate rooms, there was never dinner prepared, and I blamed myself for the failure of the relationship.

I decided to go to counselling on my own. Cathy did not want to come, but I felt I needed to make changes in my own behaviour. As well as going to counselling, I went to an anger management course, which was very helpful. Shortly after my thirtieth birthday, I made the decision to leave the marriage. I decided I would be a better father to my children if I were not in a destructive relationship. I read a lot, and learnt as much as I could from my counselling sessions.

Gradually I left the blame and guilt behind, and began to like myself again. I now understand that my anger stemmed from anxiety and stress. I didn't know how to handle either, and would shout and yell to release these feelings. I am very relieved that I am no longer in a destructive marriage. We were too young to marry; not ready for the responsibility of children, and we both had unresolved personal issues.

I strongly advocate therapy when you hit a bad patch. I have friends whose marriages have broken up, but without counselling they will go into another relationship and repeat the negative patterns.

As you can see from Jeff's story, anger was a major force in destroying his relationship. Most of us experience the emotion of anger to some degree in certain situations throughout our lives. Indeed, anger is a natural emotional response, designed to provide us with emotional and physical energy to protect us from hurt, danger and violation, frustrations and threats. The symptoms of anger manifest themselves in our bodies, our actions, facial expressions and in our minds. We all have different anger thresholds – some people are slow to anger, while others become furious with little provocation.

Many of us have not been taught how to manage our anger. We may have been told that anger is a 'bad' emotion and been encouraged to suppress our anger, to keep our cool and hide angry outbursts. We will discuss the negative effects of suppressing anger, as well as ways of handling our own anger, and anger that is directed at us.

The key to understanding anger is to accept that we all have a right to be angry. Indeed, anger can be positive, and we can learn skills to express and manage our anger. Each individual develops their own unique pattern of feeling, perceiving and responding to anger. We respond differently to the same trigger or situation, depending on our personality and history.

Do some people never express anger?

As we have said, some people are taught to suppress their anger. This anger turned inwards may reveal itself as depression.

A person may not feel safe about expressing anger towards the person who has hurt her. For example, a child may not express anger at a parent who abuses or neglects her – especially if she is dependent on that person. She blames herself or denies blame, instead of expressing her feelings to the person responsible for perpetrating the hurt or abuse.

What is the price of being nice all the time?

Certain people, especially women, try to be nice all the time. Such women can be seen as 'martyrs'. They often end up unfulfilled as they are not getting their needs met. If they do feel angry they will cry instead, or blame themselves for feeling distressed instead of expressing anger at the appropriate person.

How do our anger patterns develop?

When we were young, we were dependent on our caretakers and so less likely to express our rage at any maltreatment. Our parents may not have given us permission to express hurt or painful experiences, but we have certainly all been on the receiving end of anger. What did it feel like? Did the adults around you express their anger in a constructive or destructive way? Did you witness violence? Violence creates a pattern of repeated violence, so it is vital to understand our own experience of anger and how it developed. For only when we gain insight into how our past experiences affect our own expression of anger, can we work towards resolving destructive anger patterns.

When do we have the right to be angry?

If we are attacked, robbed, violated, hurt or cheated, we have the right to get angry. Likewise, if we are exploited, manipulated, ignored or frustrated. We may feel let down by someone who breaks a promise, or who is late. We may feel rejected or threatened. We may be abused or see others being treated badly.

All these situations can trigger an angry response – we have the right to express our anger safely and assertively. We have the right to protect ourselves from others who may be aggressive and violent, or passive and silent. If you do not respond to the anger that you feel, you may damage your physical and mental health.

Is there a pay-off for someone who is perpetually nice and ignores their angry feelings?

Some people want to be liked so desperately that they don't dare express any negative feelings such as anger. They let others get away with murder. However, each time you try to ignore abuse, offensive or unpleasant behaviour, you are indirectly encouraging it. In a way, you are being dishonest, as you are masking your true feelings.

Ironically, people who spend a large part of their lives hiding their anger with 'niceness' can become bitter and resentful, and still suffer from the physical effects of anger: muscle tension, headaches, backache and stomach aches. They may suffer from low self-esteem, and their relationships will deteriorate.

How do we learn to be more honest with our feelings?

Gradually take the risk of expressing how you feel in an appropriate way. When you realise that others can cope with your feelings, you will be increasingly willing and able to express your anger.

How can we uncover and heal childhood wounds?

Talking is always good. You may choose to confide in a friend or a professional therapist. Talk about times from your past when you experienced hurt or neglect. What did it feel like, what was happening? If your memory feels blocked, go through old photo albums. Images may trigger memories.

Ignoring unresolved issues or unfinished business in your adult relationships won't make them go away. Facing your anger is more productive. If you carry anger towards a person, you are allowing her past actions to continue hurting you in the present. By letting go of that anger, you disempower that person. Say to yourself, 'I will not allow you to hurt me any more'. You cannot change the past but you can let go of your attachment to it.

How can we express our anger in a constructive way?

The sooner you deal with angry feelings, the better. It makes sense to confront an issue when it is causing you mild irritation rather than waiting until it makes you white with rage. Be watchful of your own physiological state. If you notice yourself becoming tense, your breathing becoming shallow, and a tightness in your stomach or back, identify the trigger, then take a step back and look at the situation objectively. Ask yourself:

- What are my rights in this situation?
- Are any of my rights being violated?
- Am I in danger?
- Am I suffering from stress that may be fuelling my reaction to this situation?
- What am I afraid of?

Do you have some tips to help express anger more assertively?

Take time out to assess the situation, and then write down or rehearse in your mind a response to the issue. Some other tips to handling your anger include:

- Start positively when you address the other person. For example, 'Our friendship means a lot to me but there is something I would like to discuss ...'
- Use 'I' statements such as 'I am feeling annoyed, (irritated or angry)'.
- Be specific about why you are angry.
- Don't accuse others – own your own feelings.

- Be realistic in your accusations – don't overdramatise or threaten. Confront the behaviour that is upsetting you.
- State how you feel. For example, 'I find it hurtful when you swear at me', or 'I was upset when you criticised me in front of our friends'.
- Don't scream, shout or lose your temper. If you are upset, take some deep breaths before you speak.
- State your case rationally. If you do have an outburst, apologise.
- If the other person is verbally abusive to you, don't retaliate. Suggest you both take time out to calm down before you continue. Yelling at each other will not help resolve the issue.

If you do not confront and deal with your anger when you feel it, you may become detached and withdraw from the relationship. Denial of anger can cause resentment and depression. It will damage your health and your relationships. Learn to get in touch with your anger, express it assertively and then move on. In the same way, you need to learn to cope with anger directed towards you.

Can you describe some negative patterns of anger?

There are two kinds of anger that you may encounter. Repressed anger may come from someone with whom you are in a close relationship. Instead of expressing the angry feelings in an open way, your partner may transmit his anger more subtly. He may withdraw into silence and make it difficult for you to reconnect, or he may communicate with criticism, snide remarks or put-downs. Passive anger habits can build up over time, and if you are on the receiving end of it you may need to learn coping skills.

Observe the warning signs. Before you marry or move in with your partner, make sure you know what he does when he becomes angry or frustrated. Some people shout and yell, others go quiet, others may disappear for a while. We may not have discovered these things from dating; often we need to live at close quarters to observe responses to anger.

How should we cope with angry outbursts from others?

When we are faced with fiery anger from someone in a relationship, be it a partner, parent, boss, or friend, we may react with fear, rage or hurt. Try saying to yourself, 'This is a temporary state', 'I will not respond to this person until he has calmed down', 'I am not responsible for her feelings', 'I am determined to stay calm', 'I do not have to react with anger', or 'I have the right to protect myself'.

What is the best way to respond to an angry person?

Try to acknowledge the other person's feelings by saying, 'I understand you feel angry'. You validate her emotions and defuse the anger. You can also state how you feel. For example, 'I feel frightened when you yell loudly', or 'I'm afraid you may lose control when you become angry'.

If you have done something to upset or antagonise the other person, a simple apology works wonders. Saying, 'I'm sorry I was late', or 'I'm sorry that I could not be here for you', may be all it takes to rectify the situation.

How should we handle criticism?

Constant criticism can have a negative impact on your self-esteem and well-being. Your immediate goal should be to protect yourself by stopping the attacks. Your instinct may be to fight back or run away, but if you confront the critic by agreeing partially with him, you take the wind out of his sails. He cannot feed off your resistance.

Why and how do some women suppress their anger?

Although many women of the older generation may have been socialised to suppress their anger, many younger women also prefer to avoid confrontation. Women may be afraid to vent their feelings in case they say something they regret later. They could also be in a relationship with a potentially violent person. Fear of punishment from a partner may prevent them from displaying their anger.

THERE IS ALWAYS PAIN BEHIND ANGER

WHEN A PERSON BECOMES ANGRY WITH YOU, THINK OF THEIR ANGER AS A CONSEQUENCE OF THEIR PAIN. THIS WILL HELP YOU TO RESPOND CONSTRUCTIVELY, RATHER THAN DESTRUCTIVELY.

You may also resist expressing anger in case you are criticised or labelled. You say you are fine when you are fuming inside. By withholding you feelings, however, you are preventing your needs from being met. Perhaps you feel you can get things off your chest by talking to a friend or relative. But if you are taking out your frustrations on someone other than the person who caused you to be angry, or simply give your partner the silent treatment, you may be managing your anger in an unhealthy way. Withholding anger can create physical problems. If you become tense or worried, and develop headaches, a feeling of weakness or shakiness, eventually you may become ill or depressed.

Suppressing your anger, therefore, is not a healthy way to solve relationship problems. Try to identify what you do when you are angry:

- Do you act as though nothing has happened, keeping your feelings to yourself?
- Do you apologise even if you are right, just to keep peace?
- Do you experience intense physical symptoms, such as headaches or tightness in the stomach? Do you get nervous or shaky?

- What is the pay-off for not speaking up?
- What would you gain by expressing your feelings?

You need to engage in direct, honest communication with the target of your frustration. If you do not feel comfortable doing this, it is a good idea to role-play the scene with a friend or therapist first.

What are the positive functions of anger?

The energy generated from anger can fuel action. If we suppress this energy, we are holding ourselves back. As we have mentioned, many women feel more comfortable talking about the angry situation to a friend rather than directing the anger to the source of the problem. It feels a safer course of action.

The key is not to suppress your anger or vent your rage. It is learning to manage your anger in a constructive way. I have many clients who come to see me for help in dealing with anger. We all get mad. We need to learn how to express our anger so that we can resolve conflicts and get our needs met. Negative expression can be destructive, but positive expression releases the anger and tension. Anger has the function of protecting us from danger, in many cases physical as well as emotional. By holding onto anger we can cause both physical and emotional damage to our health.

Toolbox

- What do you do when you get mad, angry or frustrated?
- Identify your own pattern of expressing angry feelings.
- How does this behaviour make you feel? Be aware of passive anger patterns.
- When you get angry, try to work out what you are angry about.
- What fuels your anger? Learn to identify what pushes your buttons.
- Do you lose your temper? Is there another way you can handle your anger?
- If you suffered abuse of any kind in your childhood, you may still be carrying anger from that experience. Get professional help.
- Deal with angry feelings as soon as they arise.
- You do not have to respond to other people's anger with rage. Choose your response.
- Learn to manage your anger in a constructive way.

section two

Relationships

Most of us enter a relationship with the expectation that being in a union will make us happier. We expect to have our needs met, and to experience friendship, intimacy and security. Some of us may also hope that the relationship will compensate for earlier losses, take away our pain and fill the gap in our inner self. In fact, the opposite may happen. If someone with low self-esteem enters a relationship hoping that the other will magically make him feel better about himself, he will be disappointed. A relationship has a much better chance of providing joy, intimacy and security if both partners have resolved personal issues. Developing a positive sense of self is a prerequisite for being in a mutually satisfying relationship.

Once we are in a relationship, we need to examine the skills required to nurture the relationship on an ongoing basis. One of these skills is the ability to resolve differences and fight fairly. Many of us expect to know how to do this automatically. Yet often all we have to fall back on is the example we have observed in our family of origin. We may have been involved in, or observed, screaming matches or extended periods of silence where neither partner spoke to each other for days on end. Few of us had parents who dealt with their differences in a respectful way. However, you can educate yourself to learn healthy conflict resolution skills, and in so doing, enhance the quality of your relationships.

Practical exercises are provided for couples to integrate into their lives to ensure that they deal with issues in an open and constructive way. You will also learn how to negotiate what you want, fulfil your and your partner's needs and create an emotional environment that is filled with love and respect.

We examine two areas that are a constant source of conflict: money and sex. We discuss the importance of a satisfying sex life (intimacy as well as intercourse) and look at some practices that may enhance intimacy in your relationship. In the beginning, sexual attraction is strong. In fact, it may be the reason for getting together in the first place. We hope to show you how to keep alive the chemistry, connection and attraction.

Conflict around financial issues can become a very

destructive force and a source of major arguments. Few couples have serious financial discussions before they marry or move in together. Problems then emerge, and many couples do not have the skills to resolve them. We provide practical tools to deal with the financial area of our life.

Then we look at how to recognise signs that tell us a relationship is not working. Do we stay or go? We examine the decision-making process. We show you ways to minimise the pain for all involved, especially any children, if you do decide to split from your partner. Divorce is almost always traumatic, and Susie is a fierce protector of children in the divorce process. She advocates counselling so that all parties have support at this very difficult time. Parting with respect and care is possible.

Finally, we believe that one of the best things that parents can do for each other is love each other. As parents we set a powerful example to our children of what a relationship should look like. The best investment for your children's future emotional well-being is to nurture your own relationship.

chapter seven

Creating Lasting Intimacy

SARA, AGED THIRTY-ONE, CAME TO see me. She had married recently but was experiencing some conflict with her partner, Danny. They were not major issues but they were eroding the quality of their relationship.

Sara explained to me that before they married, Danny acted as though he was quite self-sufficient and wanted to help with household chores. Since they had married, he was helping less and less. What should she do? They both worked, but Danny worked longer hours and Sara worked from home.

I explained that marriage is about meeting each other's needs and pleasing each other. The key was to know each other, and understand what Danny really liked. If Sara forced him to do things he did not want to do, she was courting disaster. Dividing up household chores may work in some relationships but not in all. The goal is harmony in the relationship. Sara and Danny had to accept each other's idiosyncrasies.

Choose your fights. It is not worth creating a huge issue about every single disagreement. Give in on the areas which are less important and then you will feel more of a right to expect him to compromise on an issue which means a lot to you.

Don't see things from your perspective only. Look at the big picture and see what compromises your partner makes for you. Relationships do not have to be equal to be happy as long as one partner is not consistently giving in. Harmony can exist where there is a sense of fairness about each person's contribution. We juggle our rights and roles to achieve satisfaction.

What situations create stress in a marriage?

For a marriage to survive and thrive, a couple must develop the capacity to cope with change, and with events that may place stress on their relationship. A marriage is never static. It is a dynamic process that evolves and transforms itself over time.

Major life events such as the birth of a child and changes in career and financial stresses may put pressure on the relationship. The couple's ability to handle these events depends on the degree of love, commitment and trust they have for each other. This will influence the amount of change and tension they can handle. Individuals vary in their capacity to handle stress and change. This ability often relies on their self-worth and inner strength.

Why is it so important for couples to communicate effectively?

Every couple will go through periods in which there are problems and difficulties. In a secure relationship, the couple can weather the storms and sort out problems as they arise. However, some couples find it a challenge to express their feelings.

Where there is open, honest communication, it is possible to share a range of feelings, from love to anger. But if feelings are not revealed, this can lead to increasing tension, resentment, and dissatisfaction. Couples who avoid direct communication may rely on more covert methods to ascertain what their partner is feeling. For example, one partner is forced to interpret how the other feels from his gestures or body language. This indirect form of communication, or 'guessing', can lead to misunderstandings. It is useful to learn an open, direct form of communication, as it results in a healthier relationship.

How can a couple nurture the intimacy in their relationship?

It is very important for both individuals to be able to be themselves in a relationship. This gives each partner space to grow as an individual as well as in the marriage. In some relationships, one or both partners can become overdependent. This places considerable pressure on the other to provide for all their emotional needs. This restricts each person's capacity to be free and to be himself. There needs to be a balance between separateness and togetherness.

In order for intimacy to develop, there must be an environment in which each feels accepted and understood. Intimacy may provide a deep sense of fulfilment and belonging. The lack of intimacy may give rise to insecurity and loneliness within the relationship.

SALLY FELL IN LOVE WITH Derek, who was taken by her sweetness and charm. They married six months after they met. Derek worked for a large IT company and was transferred to Sydney from London a year after their wedding.

Sally had always been an overprotected child. Things were done for her. She was given the message that if she didn't succeed in what she was doing, there would be no repercussions. In fact, her parents enjoyed having Sally dependent on them.

It was at this point that Sally's lack of confidence became a problem. She struggled to adjust to the new environment. When she got lost while driving, she expected Derek to leave the office to come and help her out, just like her parents would have done. She felt lonely far away from her family and friends. Derek responded by becoming critical of her, constantly telling her what he expected of her in a negative rather than encouraging tone.

His criticism exacerbated her lack of confidence, leaving her even less able to cope. She found Derek increasingly angry and controlling. She was ready to return to London. It was at this stage that they came to see me. My first task was to get this young couple to communicate in a more effective manner. I defined the problems and made sure that each understood what the other was experiencing and feeling. They took turns talking and showed that they were really listening to each other.

Sally felt overwhelmed by her circumstances and needed help in breaking the problems down so that she could tackle one thing at a time. She needed encouragement, not criticism, from Derek. He needed to be patient with her. Sally needed to show him that even when things were difficult, she would keep trying. Once they were able to resolve conflicts in a more constructive manner in the therapy sessions, they were able to carry all the new skills into their day-to-day life.

What other pressures can affect a relationship?

Besides the interpersonal problems in a marriage that stem from overdependency, a lack of open communication and sexual incompatibility, external events also exert pressure. How a couple copes with these external pressures depends on the strength of their relationship and their ability to adapt to adverse circumstances. Some of these events may include ill health, problems with in-laws, parenting issues and employment patterns.

In some ways these external pressures may be easier to deal with than interpersonal problems. Partners may receive support from family and friends when they are faced with external troubles. During these times, the couple has something outside themselves to focus on. However, there are times where we may have to deal with a number of stresses simultaneously, and this can lead a couple into crisis.

What are some negative patterns of behaviour that some couples adopt to cope with difficult times?

There may be constant arguments that leave both partners feeling upset, especially if the issues are left unresolved. One or both partners may resort to constant criticism of each other. The person who criticises often does it as a way of venting his anger in a controlled manner. This makes it difficult for the other partner to respond, and avoids dealing with the underlying problem.

One or both may resort to excessive drinking as a means of coping. A form of violent behaviour may emerge, such as one partner throwing objects and/or physically assaulting the other. This is a danger signal for a relationship. Unless underlying problems are tackled, the violence may increase.

When sexual problems occur, one or both partners may begin an affair to compensate for feeling emotionally neglected in their relationship. Affairs are not always totally sexual in nature. In the next chapter we will look at the different ways of resolving these conflicts.

What are the qualities that a relationship needs to thrive?

In order for a relationship to thrive it is essential for each partner to have his or her needs met. It's as simple as that.

Could you describe the emotional needs in a relationship?

We all have a need to be loved. Often we assume that our partner knows this but we still need him to say it and show it in various ways. You may express your love in an action, such as bringing your partner a cup of tea or coffee in bed, or with an affectionate gesture or an endearing nickname.

Start the day with affection and an expression of love. This puts you in a positive mood for the day. Welcome each other at the end of each day with affection and love. Stop what you are doing for a kiss and a hug. When you connect it is so easy to continue what you are doing – cooking, talking on the phone, working on the computer – but stop. Take a few minutes to give each other some undivided attention.

We also have a need to feel needed. We like to feel that we do not come last on each other's list of priorities. Let your partner know thar you are happy that you have chosen each other as a life partner and that you would make the same choice again.

If you start your life together in this way and make a point of taking an extra five minutes each day to do little things for each other, then you are more likely to have a happy, content, loving relationship. When we come home and our young child runs to hug and kiss us, we feel good. In a similar way, if our partner rushes to greet us with open arms instead of continuing his activity, we feel loved, wanted and appreciated.

How do we create trust in a relationship?

Some couples may have a major argument if one partner forgot to pick up the dry cleaning, for instance. If you feel you have to tell a lie to cover up something you have done, the relationship is displaying a lack of trust and honesty. Trust is a valuable quality in a relationship.

To have total trust means other needs have to be met first. You have to feel secure in expressing yourself honestly. If you feel you need to hide issues for fear of being verbally abused, it is difficult to be open and trusting. Trust relates to many aspects of a relationship. The first thing that comes to mind is fidelity. You need to be aware of each other's expectations with regard to the dynamics of your relationship with the opposite sex.

I know I get jealous if I see my husband deep in conversation with a woman for a long time. I'm much better now, but early on in our relationship I felt less secure. A few months ago my husband had a personal trainer. She was a very sexy twenty-two year-old and he is fifty. She would ring at all hours to confirm their exercise sessions. When I saw him with her at the beach I couldn't look, I was overcome with jealousy.

I decided to solicit the family's help, and over a family dinner I shared my dilemma. The family took a great angle. They persuaded my husband that the trainer was more interested in his wallet than his fitness and that sowed the seeds that soon ended his relationship. Of course this was not serious, but it did highlight what it may feel like to be jealous. I always tell my husband I trust him, but I don't always trust other women.

I had another funny experience a while back. I found an American Express receipt next to my husband's bed one day when I was tidying up. It was from a florist and was for $50. I hadn't received flowers from my husband for months and I couldn't imagine to whom he needed to send flowers. My mind started to imagine that there was another woman. I could hardly wait for my husband to come home. I was very upset by the time he walked in.

NURTURE YOUR FRIENDSHIP

SPEAK TO EACH OTHER THE WAY YOU WOULD TO A FRIEND WHOSE FRIENDSHIP MEANS A LOT TO YOU. BE AS GENEROUS AND UNSELFISH WITH YOUR PARTNER AS YOU ARE WITH YOUR CLOSE FRIENDS.

After dinner I asked him straight out: 'Who did you send these flowers to?' 'My secretary,' he said. 'She was in hospital due to a miscarriage and I sent her a bouquet of flowers.' I was so relieved. However, it gave me a taste of that jealous wife syndrome!

Different couples have varying levels of tolerance for interaction with the opposite sex. Some partners may be comfortable with the other partner going for a coffee with a friend of the opposite sex; in another relationship this would not be acceptable. It is important not to be paranoid, and to be relaxed about a certain level of social interaction. Discussing the issues openly and setting parameters that you both feel comfortable with is the best way forward. Be sensitive to each other's feelings.

In modern life, the lack of structure in relationships contributes to the high percentage of divorce. Couples need to have a clear understanding of expectations with regard to their interaction with the opposite sex, old flames and ex-partners. In my experience, open marriage has never worked, even if both partners agreed to it at some stage. Often one partner feels forced into agreeing to an open relationship for fear of losing the partner who is keen to try it. If you are courting infidelity you are playing with fire. Fidelity needs to be discussed prior to marriage to ensure both of you have similar values and expectations. With an issue as vital as fidelity, you cannot afford to have different ideas from your partner.

If you are having an affair and your partner finds out, you will destroy the element of trust in your relationship. It takes a long time and a lot of hard work to rebuild that trust, so it is worth giving serious thought to an extra-marital relationship before you embark on one. Is it worth the hurt you will cause your partner?

Are there any other significant areas in a relationship where trust is particularly important?

Trust is very important with regard to financial issues and money matters. You must be able to trust your partner's word. Trust and honesty go hand in hand – in order to have trust, there needs to be honesty. You need to feel you can be honest and open, even if you are admitting something your partner may be upset about. You must not be afraid of an explosion if you admit to a minor misdemeanour. For example, if you bought a new pair of shoes with money that was earmarked for saving, you should be able to confess without fearing major repercussions.

Can you change someone?

It has been said that women marry men with the hope they will succeed in changing them, and men marry in the hope that their wives will not change. The truth is you cannot change anyone except yourself, and even this is not easy. You need to feel that your partner loves you for who you are. No-one is perfect.

We tend to love our children unconditionally, but it is more difficult to give the same unconditional love and acceptance to our partners. Why is that?

We do tend to love our children unconditionally, but we may not like some of their behaviour. When our children are young we can teach them to change their behaviour and help them develop desirable qualities. When we marry, our partner's character is already developed. We should never enter a long-term relationship with the aim of changing that person. That attitude can only lead to disappointment. Instead, we must learn to respect each other's differences and enjoy our partner's uniqueness.

What about the need for respect?

You need to respect your partner for his individuality and understand that his needs may be different from yours. If you want a healthy relationship it is essential that there is a solid friendship. You need to be able to enjoy each other's company, laugh together and have fun. It is not vital that you share all the same interests but it is important to have some mutual or shared activities.

You cannot expect your partner to satisfy all your social, intellectual and spiritual needs. That creates too much dependency in your relationship. By having outside friendships and stimulation, you can bring new ideas and vitalise your relationship.

Earlier you mentioned physical needs. Can you expand on this?

That's the one area where each partner has a responsibility to meet the other's needs. Intimacy is so much more than the sexual relationship. Physical needs can be satisfied in many ways, and by asking clients how many times a week they have sex, I would be no closer to assessing their level of intimacy.

Repeated rejection of your partner's sexual advances gives the message that you find him undesirable. This is not good for your relationship. However, when one partner is stressed, tired or physically unwell, making love may be the last thing on his mind. If your partner does reject your advances, try to understand what may be causing his behaviour before you feel rejected.

What is real intimacy in a relationship?

To me, real intimacy is lying in bed snuggled up to my partner with my head resting on his shoulder, lying as close as possible and sharing our thoughts and feelings. Intimate actions include being hugged and held, being touched and caressed as well as being kissed. For some couples, intimacy includes holding hands, laughing together, taking a bath together or giving each other a massage.

If you have true intimacy you will respect each other's sexual needs, even though your sexual desire may not be the same. This does not mean that every time one partner wants to make love, the other has to respond. It does mean, however, that sometimes you will comply even if you are not in the mood. At other times, your partner will make love to you even if he does not feel like it. If there are tremendous differences in the sexual needs of a couple, one person may be left frustrated and dissatisfied. This will create problems in the relationship. It has been said that if there are problems on the physical side of a relationship, the problem assumes ninety per cent importance. With most couples, if there is a healthy, happy sexual relationship, the sexual part of the relationship only assumes ten per cent importance. It is the glue that cements a relationship. If it is working, the relationship proceeds smoothly in all areas. If not, it can destroy or poison the relationship.

How can a couple meet each other's spiritual needs?
The key word is respect. Today, many couples do not share the same religion or spiritual practices. What is important is to respect and acknowledge each other's individual beliefs even when they are different from yours. You may even participate in each other's religious practices. When you do marry someone from a different religion or someone who is more observant than you, it is important to discuss expectations and any compromises that need to be made prior to marriage.

What about social needs?
With regard to social needs, it is essential that there is a balance between time as a couple, alone, and time with friends and family. You need time alone as a couple when you can stop being parents and just enjoy each other's company. It is also healthy to have some separate friends that you see on a one-on-one basis, as long as you do not give priority to friends instead of your partner. Arrange activities with other couples and vary what you do. Once every three months have a weekend away with your partner, so that you have quality time together.

What about the need for security?
You need to know that your partner will stand by you and support you in times of crisis, whether it is an emotional, financial or health matter. You need to feel that your partner is loyal and committed, and that he will not take flight and run at the first sign of trouble. You want to feel that if there is a disagreement, your partner will be there to work through it with you. You need to feel your relationship will not be put at risk if you have a difference of opinion or experience a crisis. You need to feel secure enough to know that your relationship can withstand some conflict. Your partner should provide a soft place to shelter and an escape from outside pressure. You need to be there for each other in a non-critical and understanding way.

How do we find out which area of our relationship is in trouble?
I have identified the needs in a relationship, as many couples are not aware of them. They experience problems but don't know which area of their relationship is in trouble. This 'needs analysis' is a bit like a diagnostic tool. We can identify the need for security, social, sexual, emotional, spiritual, financial needs and the need for intimacy and companionship

The first step is understanding what needs can be met in your relationship. The next step is sharing those needs with your partner. Don't expect your partner to read your mind.

Why would one partner refuse to meet the other partner's needs?
Your partner may not meet your needs because they conflict with his own. Or he may not listen to your needs because he is preoccupied with his own issues. He may be self-centred or selfish and not considerate of what you need.

Sometimes a person will not meet his partner's needs because he is afraid of being hurt. When people open themselves up to risk they become vulnerable. If they have experienced rejection they may find it painful to take that risk again. If you find your partner always puts his own needs first, make sure you get therapy.

We come together in relationships for a myriad of reasons. We may fall madly in love, desire a family, connect for companionship or friendship, or even get together out of financial need. Whatever our initial motivations, the future of our relationship depends on our ability to meet each other's needs in a mutually satisfying way so that the relationship can grow and evolve.

What do you do if your partner has a bad temper?
If your partner has a short fuse and goes off the deep end you have to nip it in the bud. If you allow him to get away with it, you set the pattern. You have to let him know the very first time that he loses his temper that you feel hurt, upset and insulted.

He may be unaware that he is being offensive. He may have grown up in a household where shouting at each other was the pattern of communicating. He will consider this acceptable behaviour. I would suggest individual therapy for him.

Everyone has to learn how to cope with anger in a constructive way. We learn how to express anger in our families of origin and then we tend to repeat those patterns. Or you may come from a family where anger was suppressed. When someone was upset they withdrew and became tight-lipped. Stony silence can be just as frustrating and hurtful as verbal abuse. You may come from a family of volatile tempers where your parents did a lot of screaming, shouting and plate throwing.

None of these behaviours is constructive. If your partner does shout at you, wait until he calms down and say, 'Let's stop here and continue talking when we have both calmed down'.

Verbal abuse is as damaging as a physical blow. Don't lower yourself to the other person's standards. You can also look at your own behaviour and see if you can say things in a less provocative way. For example, instead of saying, 'You're wrong', rephrase, and say, 'I see things differently'.

What do you do if your partner is stubborn?

A stubborn person is usually a bit insecure. He finds it hard to back down. It makes him feel as if he is losing and the other person is winning. It becomes a power game to hold onto his position. He becomes his own worst enemy.

If you do have a stubborn partner, choose a time when you are both feeling good and discuss the issues. Always speak with 'I' messages. For example, 'When you refused to go to my parents for dinner, I felt very upset. I felt you were not considering my needs at all. I was looking forward to having dinner with my family. My parents were insisting that we come. You were insisting that we didn't. I felt like the meat in the sandwich. Can we find a way to work this out?'

What doesn't work is to beg, plead and cajole, because the stubborn person will only get more entrenched in his position. You also need to give him a way out so that he can look like a hero instead of a defeated weakling. Create an option that gives him a chance to change his mind, and then don't butt in. After all, we all have some issues that we are stubborn about.

What do you do if your partner is moody?

Moodiness can be a deliberate form of sulking. but it may also be a response to stress experienced during the day. Sulking is a form of passive–aggressive behaviour. Instead of yelling, the person expresses their anger by withdrawing. This is difficult for their partner to handle as it negates them and is hurtful. Try to learn to differentiate between a quietness which may be due to stress, and deliberate disconnection which is designed to hurt you.

Often our response to a partner's moodiness is, 'What have I done wrong?' We need to get out of the habit of owning a problem that is not ours. Sometimes things happen at work and our partner gets upset. Asking direct questions may not work. Perhaps ask, 'You seem to be unhappy. Is there something you want to share?' If your partner says 'no', just say, 'That's fine. I'm here if you want to talk'.

Often my partner comes home upset or stressed and really doesn't want to talk. He wants to relax on the couch and watch sport on TV. My best course of action is to give him the space until he wants to connect.

By doing that you are respecting his need to unwind. My husband likes to come home and disappear into the shower. This gives him an opportunity to unwind and relax. Then we talk. This enables him to shed the stress of his workday. I used to come home from work and shut myself up in my room and do a crossword puzzle. It distracted me from the stresses of the hospital and enabled me to mentally unwind.

What do you do if your partner is critical of everything you do?

If your partner is critical, be honest with yourself. Is his criticism valid? Can you do something about it? If you feel the criticism is not valid, choose your time carefully and discuss the issue. Take turns to speak and really listen to each other without interrupting. You may say, 'I feel very upset when you criticise my cooking, my clothes or my friends'.

We need to be able to differentiate between deliberate put-downs and constructive criticism. Some people become very defensive and can't recognise or even accept constructive criticism. It is helpful in a relationship to have an open mind and, most importantly, to listen to each other without feeling defensive. Create an environment where it is safe to say anything.

What do you do if the same issues keep coming up?

The bottom line is that a relationship is a partnership. Treat your partner the way you would like to be treated. If there are issues that keep repeating themselves over and over again I would suggest going to a therapist to resolve them. The most important thing in a relationship is to have skills to resolve problems; otherwise they hang around and poison a relationship. Relationships require hard work and they change as circumstances around you change.

Couples often have trouble listening to each other. This leads to there being unresolved issues that undermine the relationship. Stepping into your partner's shoes and understanding how he feels will bring about a positive change. Once your partner validates your feelings and you know he has listened to you, much of the hurt and anger dissolves.

Sometimes one partner feels they are doing all the giving and the other is doing all the taking. While this may be true, it is often a perception of one of the partners. Couples need to discuss how they could achieve a sense of fairness in their relationship, and a balance of give and take.

Toolbox

Myths about healthy relationships

- *You have to have the same interests to have a successful relationship.*
  You should have some mutual interests. The important things you share, however, are your relationship, your home and your children. You can still have a happy marriage with some different pursuits.

- *A great relationship is all about sex.*
  Sex is not everything, but if you have a good sex life with your partner, you can move on to other aspects of your relationship. However, if you have problems in that area it becomes all-consuming. Sex is not just intercourse. It is cuddling, touching, kissing, hugging, all the physical things from sensual to affectionate.

- *A great relationship is one where a couple never argues.*
  Arguments can help your relationship to grow. The issue is not whether you fight but how you fight.

- *True passion will last forever.*
  It doesn't. You have to work at creating situations that maintain the romance. Go away for weekends without the children, go out for dinner with your partner somewhere

quiet, light aromatic candles in the bedroom. Like everything else in life, marriage has to be worked out

- *Your partner should satisfy all your needs.*
  It is totally impossible for one person to fill all your needs. We all need a variety of people in our lives for friendship, affection and stimulation as well as for sharing different activities. Each person should have space, separate friends and some special interests. Don't try to merge into one. Once you become too dependent, you find it difficult to function without your partner. If you demand that one person meet all your emotional needs, you put enormous pressure on that person.

- *Partners will change once they marry.*
  This is another unrealistic expectation that women in particular have, often marrying with the intention of changing their spouse. Men hope their wives will never change! Both spouses are sorely disappointed. The things that annoy you about your partner now will annoy you more in five years' time. If flaws or bad habits disappear, it's a bonus, but don't count on it.

- *If couples get married, all problems will disappear.*
  We are nurtured on the Cinderella fantasy of 'happily ever after', but it is an unrealistic expectation. Every relationship has its ups and downs; disagreements and conflict are an integral part of any relationship. The key is to learn the skills to deal with problems.

chapter eight

Fighting Fairly

WHEN ROSS AND DIANE FIRST got together almost ten years ago, Ross was forty-one and Diane was thirty-nine. They each had two children from a previous marriage.

Ross and Diane's relationship was clearly a minefield of potential problems. When they first came to me they had been married for a year and they were struggling with a number of issues.

The first area that we tackled was their inability to fight fairly. Their disagreements followed a predictable pattern. Ross would get upset about something. Diane would ask him what was wrong. He would say nothing, but stop talking. Diane would persist and ask him to discuss what was wrong and he would say, 'I have nothing to share, I don't feel like talking'. This would go on for a day or two. Their normal daily interaction would come to an abrupt halt.

By this stage Diane would be very upset and she would withdraw. By this time Ross would be over his issue but be faced with Diane's hurt and anger. When Diane became very angry, Ross would threaten to leave and Diane would feel upset and insecure.

The problems that exist between Ross and Diane have a number of sources. Ross feared revealing his vulnerability and exposing his true feelings. He also had an inability to express his anger. Diane, while having a need for intimacy and communication, also struggled to express her anger and her own vulnerability. As they had similar problems when a conflict arose, these issues created a distance between them that was too great to overcome without help. Once we had established a background to their relationship, we were able to make a number of agreements, which would help them to resolve future conflicts and which they agreed to honour.

- If either of them got upset about something they were allowed three to four hours to cool down or take time out. After that period they were obligated to discuss the issue and listen to each other.
- They would take turns in establishing contact. If Ross did it at the last disagreement, Diane would do it the next time. This would stop either of them feeling that they always had to give in or make the first move.
- On no account was the silence and not speaking to go on for more than four hours.
- Neither of them would be permitted to threaten the other with leaving. These threats create a great deal of insecurity. It also means that the relationship is not a safe place to express feelings.
- I also encouraged them to become aware of issues before they became overwhelming and to discuss them.
- With regard to each other's children, I suggested the biological parent had regular one-on-one time with his or her own children.
- I encouraged the step-parent not to interfere in the relationship of the biological parent and their children, especially in the financial arena.
- I explained the benefits of having time together as a couple without the four teenagers.

Within months their relationship improved. They reported to me that their disagreements were becoming less frequent and that they were resolving them more quickly. This gradually strengthened their bond and deepened their love and friendship, as there was less hurt and pain.

Choose your fights. It is not worth making a huge issue about every single disagreement. Give in on the areas which are less important and then you will feel more of a right to expect your partner to compromise on an issue which means a lot to you.

Arguments are a part of every relationship. Conflict is not only normal, but necessary. If couples do not have the tools to resolve conflict, no matter how much they love each other, their relationship will gradually deteriorate. We can, however, learn to fight fairly. In order to do this, both parties have to be willing to sit down and discuss the problem with the aim of resolving it. If couples don't resolve issues as they occur, small issues will fester into big resentments that will undermine the relationship. You may discover that you and your partner have opposing arguing styles; one of you may withdraw, the other may be prone to fits of temper. One of you avoids confrontation and the other is keen to tackle issues head on. In this chapter we will learn to explore healthy ways to resolve conflict and settle arguments.

What is the best way to prevent an argument?

Arguments occur when there is a conflict of interest. Most arguments start with an issue or problem that is discussed. When agreement cannot be reached, the discussion escalates into an argument. Arguments within a relationship start to take a predictable pattern. Most of us can see the warning signs. We think to ourselves, 'here we go again'. We each have triggers that set us off; things that push our buttons and make us more likely to lose our cool. If we understand this process, we can take care when we want to have a sensitive discussion that may provoke strong emotions.

Timing is very important when we want to resolve an issue. Don't start a serious discussion with your partner when he has just come home from work, tired and stressed. Instead, ask him at a later date if he could set time aside to discuss certain issues. You could say, 'Could we create some time this weekend to talk about some things that have come up?'

Start with endearments; be caring and loving. If you intend to stay in your relationship you want caring, warmth and affection. So instead of being aggressive, choose a positive tone of voice and non-confrontational language. If you are aggressive and attack your partner, he will automatically become defensive or attack back. You could say, 'There is something that has been troubling me. Could we find a time when we will not be disturbed to try to resolve it?'

Do you think it's a good idea to choose a location other than home? I like the idea of a coffee shop or a walk in the park.
This may work well for you, but I choose my lounge room, as I feel it is a place of civilised discussion and conflict resolution. We treat each other with respect while we talk. The location matters less than the tone we use with each other. If you don't feel safe with your partner as you think he may lose his temper, a public place may help to keep the discussion under control. If that still does not feel comfortable, set up a meeting with a therapist so that you have a third person present.

How many of your clients have good conflict resolution skills when they come to you?
Very few, but hopefully a lot more by the time they leave! Conflict resolution is an important process that is practised in therapy, providing the tools to have a constructive argument.

Is there anything we should avoid doing when we are having an argument?
One of the most important things to do is to stick to the topic. Write the topic down. Don't deviate, go into the past or bring up other issues. If one of you shifts from the topic, just gently intervene and say 'That's not the issue'. Try to use 'I' messages, owning your feelings instead of attacking the other person: 'When you say X, I feel Y because Z'. For example, 'When we went out for dinner with friends you criticised me. I felt embarrassed because you were putting me down'.

Another basic rule of fighting fair is that you should attack the problem and not the person. The aim should be not that you get your way but that it ends up being a win–win situation. If one person has a stronger personality and frequently manages to have her own way, then resentment can build up.

These are some of the things to avoid when you are having an argument.

- There is a tendency to be thinking about your reply before your partner stops talking, instead of listening. Try to break that habit. If you listen with an open mind, you may hear your partner more clearly and be more receptive. Have a pen and a paper handy. If something comes into your mind, jot down a memo and you can deal with it when it's your turn to talk. You will then not have to interrupt your partner out of fear of forgetting what you wanted to say. Interruption shows you are not really listening.
- No name-calling. It's very tempting, especially if you feel hurt or angry, to call your partner names, but it makes your partner defensive. It's insulting. Attack the problem, not the person. Another thing that arises when we get emotional, angry or frustrated is that we begin to speak in a negative tone of voice. If you secretly tape yourself at these times you will become aware that your tone is offensive. Instead of yelling, use a nice gesture or touch the other person. Have a mutual agreement prior to the conversation.
- Don't use put-downs, sarcasm or accusations. Don't say 'always' or 'never'. For example, 'You always ignore me when I talk to you and you never take me to the movies'. Neither of these is completely true, and it takes away from the present. Don't bring up the past. Remember the topic of conversation and focus closely.
- Don't blame the other person. It takes two to tango. Accept responsibility for your role in the problem. Don't go off at a tangent. Don't threaten, make excuses or try to get even.

Above all, listen to what the problem is for your partner. Focus on the things you can change rather than your partner's faults. Be solution-focused. If you find that either of you has a tendency to interrupt, it may be a good idea to get a timer and set it for ten minutes. Take turns, with the aim of giving both of you an opportunity to share your thoughts and feelings.

A few years ago my son went to a personal development group and he came back with a red velvet heart. The idea is that the person who holds the heart can talk without interruption.

That's a great idea. You could use the heart or the timer. Make sure you don't raise your voice. If you lower your voice your partner is more likely to listen. When I was working at the hospital as a social worker, there was one professor who everyone feared because he could tear strips off you. When he said to me in a very low, quiet voice, 'Mrs Wise ...' I started to shake. I had to strain to listen to what he was saying.

I have taught many of my clients to lower their voices. It actually works better because you need to concentrate to listen. When someone yells, you want to put your hands over your ears to block the noise. You are less likely to listen.

Why is therapy so effective in these situations?

Unfortunately these skills are not taught in high school. Even when we become aware of them, it is not easy to put then into practice when emotions are running high. When an objective, third person is present, she can help you stick to the rules of the game and teach you how to fight fairly.

Is it sometimes important to let things go rather than have an argument?

Yes – remember, you don't always have to be right. Choose issues that are really important to you so that you can expect your partner to respect how you feel. Often we have a heated argument and a few days later we have forgotten what we argued about. Many issues are not worth arguing about.

When I raised my children I taught them what was acceptable, and the guidelines were very clear. It was very rare that they wanted to do something that I felt strongly about. When I did say they weren't allowed to do something, they did not argue with me. I very rarely had to say 'no'. The shock of saying 'no' stunned them to such an extent that they accepted it. They knew it meant a lot to me and they gave in without an argument.

When I married for the second time, I faced a different scenario. Early in our relationship my husband and I had a dispute. We were invited to one of his friend's children's wedding. The invitation said 'Dinner Suit/Black Tie'. He refused to wear a dinner suit. I said, 'Darling, it means a lot to me', and assumed he would give in, just like my children would have done, and comply with my wishes. Instead, his reply was, 'You brought up your children but you didn't bring me up. It means a lot to me not to wear a dinner suit'. So in the future we agreed to compromise. On that occasion we decided not to go to the function but sent a beautiful gift instead. Over the years I agreed to accept as few invitations as possible where a dinner suit had to be worn.

JULIE, FORTY-THREE, AND STEPHEN, FORTY-FIVE, were having marital problems.

They had been married for eighteen years and had two teenage children. Both parents had very demanding jobs that required them to work long hours. They argued constantly. Julie said the arguments were caused by Stephen's heavy drinking and his verbally abusive behaviour when he had had several drinks too many. As a result of all the arguments they grew apart, no longer enjoying going out together.

After two weeks of therapy, Julie found out that Stephen had recently had an affair. My condition for continuing to work with them was that Stephen had no more contact with the other woman.

After two months of therapy, there were tremendous changes in their relationship. Previously Stephen had attributed the problems to Julie's nagging and to the amount of time her work required. Julie accepted that she had contributed to their marital problems and was prepared to make necessary changes. Stephen recognised that his drinking was a problem. Since cutting back on his alcohol intake, Julie no longer nags, and life is much more peaceful.

IT TAKES A BIG PERSON TO ADMIT THEY ARE WRONG

WHEN YOU HAVE DONE SOMETHING WRONG OR SAID SOMETHING HURTFUL, ADMIT IT AS SOON AS POSSIBLE AND ASK FOR FORGIVENESS. ASK YOURSELF, 'WOULD I RATHER BE RIGHT OR HAPPY?'

In order to rekindle the romance in their marriage, we gradually added some structured activities to enable them to enjoy each other's company once more. At first it was taking the dog for a walk together after dinner. They were also to make every effort to speak to each other the way they would want to be spoken to. With new tasks structured gradually into their life, Julie and Stephen's marriage began to improve. I noticed they became more affectionate with each other. There is still work to be done, but they are much happier than the couple I first met on the verge of divorce.

That's an inspiring story, but what if your partner breaks all the rules of fair fighting?

In these situations you may need a therapist to establish some guidelines. If your relationship is in such a bad way that you practise very few effective communication skills, it will fall apart without professional help. A vital component of any relationship is respect. You need to respect each other's feelings. This respect is reflected in how you talk, how you listen and how you respond to your partner's emotions. Never dismiss something that is important to your partner.

Sometimes couples have the same argument over and over again like a rusty old record. What should they do?

When you have an ongoing issue, a more definitive structure is required to resolve differences. The Prepare/Enrich Program suggests ten steps to follow. I recommend this model, which can help couples resolve conflicts.

- Set a time and place for discussion.
- Define the problem or disagreement topic.
- Describe how you each contribute to the problem.
- List unsuccessful past attempts to resolve the issue.
- Brainstorm all possible solutions.
- Discuss and evaluate these possible solutions.
- Agree to try one of these solutions.
- Detail the actions that each of you needs to take to work towards this solution.
- Set up another meeting to discuss your progress.
- Reward each other as you each take steps towards the solution.

It's important to realise that conflicts arise in every single relationship. The key to a healthy relationship is how these conflicts are resolved. If they remain unresolved, they can poison the relationship.

When we enter a relationship we often model the problem-solving style that we observed in our families. If they were dysfunctional, we may repeat the negative behaviour. Think about how your parents solved problems. Did they yell at each other? Were there long periods of silence where they did not talk to each other? Did they throw things at each other? Become aware of any negative or destructive behaviour you may be repeating and find more positive ways to resolve issues.

Can you give us an example of an effective problem-solving technique?

Let's use a simple example, which involves a couple planning a holiday. She wants to go on a beach holiday where she can enjoy sun, sand and blue skies. He wants to go on a skiing holiday because skiing is his passion. They need to sit down and brainstorm a few possible solutions. This may involve different suggestions. They may take separate holidays or they may alternate – one year going skiing and the following year having a beach holiday.

How will this get them closer to a solution? Well, I have often found by really understanding the other's point of view, one will say, 'Let's go on your holiday, and next year we'll go on mine'. If this doesn't happen, I suggest flipping a coin.

Most couples fight the wrong way. They see every argument as a battleground. One of them must win and the other must lose. What you need to focus on is a win for the relationship. Try to move away from the need for one of you to be right. If she beats him into submission, he will feel resentful. If she gives in all the time she will feel powerless. When you want to win you get desperate. You may make threats to leave, separate or end the relationship. Every time you get into a power struggle, you put the relationship at risk.

How can both partners win?

First of all, you need to discover the real issue you are fighting about. For example, you may have a man who wants to control and dominate. He may be threatened by his wife's independence. If she did what he required she would be severely limiting her life. She wants her husband to see her as an equal, not as a child. The more he tries to control her, the further she moves away from him.

It is vital that a couple shifts away from the power struggle. As Dr Phil McGraw says in his book, *Relationship Rescue*, 'When you put your relationship in a win–lose situation your relationship is guaranteed to lose. If one of you says, "I'm going to do what I want," you are going to alienate the other. If you make threats to leave you are playing with fire. In order to turn this around from a win–lose situation to a win–win situation you need to find your points of agreement'.

How do you do that?

Focus on what you agree on. In reality you probably agree on lots of things. By focusing on what you agree on you are switching from negative to positive. I always ask both partners, 'Is this marriage worth saving? Are you both prepared and willing to work on the marriage?'

We then make a list of all the things that the couple does agree on. This may be how you see yourself as parents, your values and beliefs or your work ethic. The areas you agree on form the foundation for overcoming the areas you disagree on. Isolate the few things you feel differently about. Often when we have an argument we become tunnel-visioned and can only see the negatives ahead. We need to focus on our strengths as a couple – this gives us the motivation to move forward.

That seems so obvious, yet I never thought of it. When we argue with our partners we become obsessed by the issue in front of us and it becomes blown out of proportion. What else can we do to create a win–win scenario?

Be specific about what you need. You cannot fulfil each other's needs unless you know what they are. You also need to work out what behaviour you need to change. Make a list of your needs. This list can save your marriage. You may need to make some changes in your relationship to improve your marriage. You can't have a bad marriage unless you have a lifestyle that supports a bad relationship. If you make changes that underpin your lifestyle, you will change the relationship. Both partners need to know they are each other's number one priority.

By eliminating stress and chaos, and creating order in your day-to-day life, you will improve the quality of your relationship. Develop your own plan to make time for each other. Get specific about what you will do. Look each other in the eye and commit to these changes. Decide to live the plan. For example, three times a week before dinner have a drink together and chat for half an hour. Take the phone off the hook so that you are not interrupted.

Always try to isolate the issue in a conflict. Be as specific as possible. Often the issue is a need that is not being met. When needs are not being met in a relationship it starts to go downhill. The relationship will only work if both of you consider each other in making your demands. Negotiate a way for both of you to get more of what you want.

Can you give an example of a specific issue that can be resolved?

A woman may ask her partner to spend more time with her and their children. The husband may say, 'I am out all day working for you. I can't spend more time with you'. She may reply, 'I need you to bring home more than money. I need you to bring home emotional, spiritual and social income so that we can interact as adults. I don't want to use you as a pay cheque. I want you. I need more of your time'.

This is a situation when both partners are right. She has every right to ask for more of his time and to have more of her emotional needs met. On the other hand, if the husband is working long hours to support his family, then the negotiations for time spent together need to be done with an understanding of his needs as well. He also needs to take time out for himself. If both partners enter the discussion with an attitude of wanting to meet each other's needs and listen to each other, there is a greater chance of finding a solution.

Should you give in to keep the peace?

In situations where one partner gives in or even caves in to get short-term peace, the relationship suffers. The partner who regularly gives in eventually becomes disempowered and resentful. It is important to come up with a solution that works. It doesn't matter who is right; find something that works. Ask yourself, 'Do I want to be right or happy?' 'What can we do so that we can both be happy?'

Ask your partner what he needs. I had a client who asked her partner for the following: 'I need you to know who I am and to accept me. I need friendship. I want you to be interested in my job and support my passion for what I do. I would like you to share in my success and celebrate with me'. In this situation, both parties were willing to work on their relationship. Through therapy they were able to become more aware of each other's needs and demonstrate this to each other, with the result that their relationship improved. The extent to which a therapist can bring about change is dependent on the effort that both parties are willing to make.

I encourage my clients to come to sessions with notebooks and to write down the issues we work through. I often give them tasks or homework to do so that they can anchor the ideas we have discussed. We need to write down a plan for making changes. All new behaviour needs to be concrete and specific. I also encourage my clients to jot down issues that arise between sessions and describe how they dealt with these. Then we can look at those examples and find a better way to resolve situations.

Toolbox

- Keep focused on the positive.
- Look for win–win solutions.
- Be specific about your needs.
- Write down an action plan.
- Find your points of agreement.
- Try to solve issues as they come up instead of storing them for a huge argument.
- Own what is yours, instead of looking to blame your partner.
- Don't fight to be right at all costs. Ask yourself, 'Do I want to be right or happy?'
- Start your sentences with 'I' and share your feelings.
- Stick to one topic per discussion. Don't try to deal with every issue at the same time.
- Poor conflict resolution can ruin your relationship faster than anything else. Unresolved issues can also undermine self-esteem and intimacy and lead to destructive habits.

chapter nine

Dealing with Sexual Issues

SHARON AND KEVIN, AGED THIRTY-TWO and thirty-six, had been married for eight years, and had two children, aged four and eighteen months. They were experiencing difficulties in their marriage, which they attributed to sexual problems.

Sharon was no longer enjoying sex and was less than enthusiastic when Kevin suggested they make love. In fact, every time Kevin put his arm around Sharon, he felt her physically withdrawing. He felt rejected, and began to withdraw emotionally.

They both agreed that this started after the birth of their second child. Sharon says:

It was a difficult birth. When we resumed sexual intercourse, I kept experiencing genital pain. My fear of that pain caused me such concern that every time Kevin showed me any affection I would feel myself withdrawing, fearing that a positive response would result in intercourse. Whereas previously I had frequently experienced multiple orgasms, I was devastated by the fact that now I found it difficult to feel aroused. Every time Kevin wanted to make love, all I could think of was the potential pain. No matter how hard I tried, I could not relax and enjoy intercourse.

Kevin became aware that Sharon would often pick an argument at bedtime to prevent Kevin making any sexual advances. Sharon was distressed that her ongoing fear of intercourse could cause her to behave like that.

They were relieved to be discussing their problems at last and were hopeful of resolving them. Sharon explained to Kevin that her lack of sexual desire was not due to any lack of love for him. She still loved him and found him very attractive. She was worried that she might lose him. She wanted to make him feel happy and appreciated, and wanted them both to have a loving sex life.

The first objective of therapy had been achieved with both of them talking about their fears, their feelings for each other, and their willingness to work together on their problem. Next, Sharon went to her gynaecologist, who excluded any physical cause for the pain she was experiencing. We then began to work on the sexual problem.

Stage One: Sharon and Kevin were told not to have sexual intercourse for six weeks. This took the pressure off Sharon, and she was able to enjoy gradual pleasuring. Initially they were only allowed to cuddle, and give each other a massage, but not touch each other's genitals. No matter how aroused they became, they were not allowed to have intercourse. This gave them an opportunity to rediscover how much pleasure they could give each other without having intercourse. They were to give each other feedback, such as 'I like that', 'softer', or 'harder'. I suggested they have two or three sessions a week, each time taking turns to pleasure each other.

Stage Two: They could now add direct pleasuring to each other's genitals, but still no intercourse. During this stage they could touch each other and show how they liked to be aroused. They had the opportunity to learn how to satisfy each other without having intercourse.

Stage Three: During this stage, they could include all the pleasuring they had discovered in the first two stages, and they could now add intercourse. I suggested they begin with Sharon on top, thereby giving her more control. Once she felt comfortable with this, they could explore other positions, always including the first two stages, so that it didn't end up just being a sexual relationship that consisted only of intercourse. Gradually their sexual relationship improved and the rest of their relationship blossomed.

Often couples experience extreme problems in their sexual relationships before they seek help. Many couples start off with a wonderfully passionate sexual relationship. After the wedding, and especially after the children arrive, it will probably deteriorate unless both partners actively nurture, prioritise and sustain their physical connection. Prevention is the best policy when it comes to sexual matters. Go for help as soon as the problems arise and you could save yourselves months or even years of pain and heartache.

How often should a couple have sex to maintain an intimate relationship?

It is a question often asked but it is irrelevant. One couple may have sex for five minutes every day. Another couple may have one intimate lovemaking session a week that lasts an hour.

The frequency of lovemaking should depend on how often both partners desire to connect, and that will vary. Couples have sex to satisfy mutual needs, to express their feelings, to relax, and for fun and recreation. It should not be too frequent for one and not too infrequent for the other. Every couple needs to establish their own patterns of lovemaking.

I often tell my clients that if they go to bed at night at the same time and lie in each other's arms chatting, spontaneous lovemaking often follows. You are creating an emotional and physical environment for a sexual connection to happen. For an intimate relationship, above all, there needs to be a mutual agreement that it is acceptable to say 'no' when you don't feel like making love. The frequency of lovemaking only becomes an issue when one partner is too demanding or the other is more rejecting. (This is not necessarily a gender issue.) The most important thing is to create the opportunity for intimacy, for you and your partner to feel valued and loved.

How important is sex in marriage?

I believe sex is the glue that cements a relationship together; not just sexual intercourse, but caressing, touching, holding, cuddling and kissing. Every magazine we open gives us instructions on sexual techniques and how to have multiple orgasms, yet none of that works unless the emotional connection between the couple is healthy. Maintain the level of touching, cuddling and kissing rather than allowing the frequency to drop and letting it gradually slip out of your relationship. If you do experience sexual problems, go to a therapist who specialises in sexual counselling.

NURTURE INTIMACY IN YOUR RELATIONSHIP

HAVE EMOTIONAL CLOSENESS, WITH CUDDLING AND ENDEARING NICKNAMES FOR EACH OTHER. IF THIS EXISTS, A LOVING SEXUAL RELATIONSHIP OFTEN FOLLOWS.

We also need to understand that the hot passion that pervades the early stages of a relationship may evolve into something else, a more comfortable, familiar connection. Electric sparks may not fly but there is something very special about making love to someone you love deeply.

The more intimate the connection between you, the more you are assured of a happy marriage. Ideally, it would be nice to aim for a one-minute hug or cuddle every single day. Some loving gesture or caress as you walk past shows you care. To me, this is more important than a bunch of flowers. Spontaneity, warmth, affection and humour will all nurture your intimacy effectively.

If we are upset or angry, we are less likely to be sexually aroused. Unresolved emotional issues may act as a huge barrier to intimate connection. Often a couple's sex life is a reflection of the emotional space or connection between them. If you are having an argument or are upset you may still be able to have sex and even orgasm, but there will not be a sense of emotional satisfaction.

Does it matter who initiates the sexual encounter?

In our egalitarian society it is desirable that both partners initiate lovemaking, but in my practice I have found that husbands initiate it more frequently.

What are the main reasons that people choose to have an affair?

I feel that an affair is usually a result of problems in the marriage that need attention, or one person in the relationship not having their needs met. If either partner goes outside the marriage to have these needs met, it creates a void in their relationship.

What often precipitates an affair is when either party has a need to prove to themselves that they are still desirable. This may be caused by a feeling of inadequacy within the individual rather than a problem in the marriage. When I see a couple in therapy, I usually see them together first and then have an individual session with each. Though others may disagree with me, I feel strongly that I should not ask someone if he is having an affair in front of his partner. If a marriage is in distress it doesn't help to compound the situation by adding lack of trust and a feeling of betrayal into it. However, I will tell the person who is having the affair that I will not work on his marriage until he puts a stop to his affair.

If one partner is having his needs met outside the marriage through an affair, then he will not be putting the necessary energy into saving or improving his marriage, and he is setting himself up for failure. If the marriage cannot be saved, then he is free to leave and continue that relationship. If the couple is to separate, I advise him to wait a while after separation before openly dating the other person in his life. This is to avoid the potentially extremely negative effect on the self-esteem of the partner who has been left. This applies even when they are already aware that there is someone else involved. For some women, it is often too painful to accept the betrayal so they live in a state of denial.

When there are children involved, it becomes even more important. Children find it very difficult to cope with the feeling that Mum or Dad has chosen that 'other' person and 'deserted us'. They may also feel resentful that their family broke up because of that other person.

Why are more women saying, 'I'm not interested', 'I'm never in the mood', 'I don't enjoy sex any more', 'I dread sex'? Is this a new epidemic? Is there something missing? Can this attitude be changed?

This loss of libido often sets in after the first child is born. As doctors recommend abstaining from sex in the first six weeks after childbirth anyway, this may be the perfect time for lying in bed cuddling with no pressure to have sex. However, having the baby in the bedroom for several months is a big turn-off for many mothers. When a woman becomes a mother, she sees it as a huge responsibility. She may become worn out, and sex is the last thing on her mind. If she is a stay-at-home mum, she may not feel her role is valued and appreciated. She loses her sense of self. If she is working full-time in a job outside the home, she will be even more exhausted and tired.

We have seen that new mothers can shy away from affection in case it leads to sex. Other reasons that turn women off sex are having a colicky baby and waking frequently at night to breastfeed. Sleep deprivation is slow torture and the exhaustion it brings is a big problem when it comes to sex. Postnatal depression also turns many women off sex.

A husband needs to be understanding at this time and not put pressure on his wife. If a woman does not have to fear that every cuddle will automatically lead to intercourse, then warmth and intimacy can be maintained. When the baby is a little older, a couple's normal lovemaking pattern can resume.

The husband has to appreciate what his partner's needs are at this time. The woman needs to feel that her husband cares about her, that he is supportive and that he respects her role. If a man is abusive, critical or derogatory towards his wife, the atmosphere will not be conducive to a harmonious sexual relationship. Some women give in to their husbands' sexual demands in order to avoid an argument. This does not make them feel good. In this situation a woman would feel more empowered if she resisted her husband's overtures until he treated her with more respect.

A negative sex life can spin everything out of control. Both partners need to take responsibility for what is happening. There is no point in one person acting like a victim. A few sessions of therapy could change your life. If your partner is not interested in going to therapy, go on your own. It is not ideal, but by changing some of your own actions, your partner will respond differently.

How can a woman prevent her loss of interest in sex when trying to raise a young family?

Work hard at maintaining intimacy. Get a babysitter as often as possible. Try to go out together a few times a month. Once you push your partner away, he will feel rejected. Some women agree to have sex but ask their partner to get it over with as soon as possible. The message she is giving him is that other chores are more important than he is and that she won't enjoy it. The more you avoid sex, the more of a barrier it becomes.

You can get intimacy back with willingness and hard work. The best way is prevention – don't let the intimacy disappear in the first place. If you get only one thing out of this book, let it be this – treasure your intimate connection. Nurture your sexual relationship in all its forms and don't let other things become more important.

A toddler in your bed can also be detrimental to a healthy sexual relationship, especially as many women feel they can't make love in front of their child. Try to keep the toddler in his own bed. Once you let him in with you, it will be harder to stop.

As your children get older, teach them to respect privacy. Instil in them the need to knock on a door if it is closed. This enables the parents to continue their relationship in the comfort of privacy. It is vital that a couple preserves its relationship as lovers, separate from their role of parents. In fact, the best thing parents can do for their children is show them that they feel affection for each other, and that their relationship matters. You are not neglecting your children by preserving your intimate connection with your partner.

Maybe some women just don't feel sexy any more.

Yes, that is sometimes the situation. A husband should play a major role in giving his partner compliments and making her feel good, but the woman also has to take responsibility. If you've had a baby recently, it is important not to neglect yourself – make sure you indulge yourself with little pleasures that make you feel good.

What about the romantic touches – flowers, candles and candlelit dinners?

In reality these are idealistic expectations, not helped by Hollywood's romanticised view of marriage. These things may help a woman's self-esteem in the short term, but what is much more important in the long term is a couple's mutual respect. I saw one couple recently where it was the husband who needed more affection and nurturing; the wife wanted an active involvement in the family finances and more independence. Once they took each other's needs into account the marriage improved greatly.

Sexual needs are no different from other requirements. Disregarding or negating each other's needs will have a serious negative effect on the relationship. Be prepared to articulate your needs, to validate your partner's needs and take them on board. Don't expect your partner to read your mind.

Are women who withhold sex ultimately punishing themselves as much as their partners?

Perhaps some women are. But the reality is that if a woman doesn't allow herself to be open and vulnerable in a sexual relationship, she doesn't feel whole in herself. She may blame her partner for not satisfying her but, in fact, she may need counselling if she wants a satisfying sexual relationship.

When I work with couples who have relationships that are not functioning well in the sexual area, I give them exercises that help them get in touch with their sensuality, eroticism and pleasure. I encourage them to spend time giving each other massages, stroking and pleasuring without having sex. They learn more about what each other wants and gradually their sexual desire for each other is rekindled. I believe we should get as much pleasure out of pleasing each other as we experience ourselves.

Some couples may find it a turn-on to watch a sexy video. If you want variety and excitement in your lovemaking, this is acceptable, as long as you both feel comfortable with what the other suggests. One partner must not force the other to do things against their will.

It is important for couples to maintain warmth and friendship, so that when passion ebbs, something more long-lasting and meaningful is there to support the relationship. This comes from sharing your dreams, goals and building a life together. Emotional security is part of this process. You can count on being there for each other, and friendship and familiarity take the place of passion comfortably.

How does your partner feel if you constantly reject him?

When a woman does not want to have sex with her partner, she should put herself in her partner's shoes. How would she feel if she wanted to make love and she was rejected? She would feel unloved, unattractive and insecure. If you do have young children, find time to get a babysitter or farm the children out so that you can spend time alone together. Recapture your husband/wife relationship.

Remember, having a satisfying sex life does not depend on a perfect body, athletic prowess or innate sex appeal. You need skills that you can acquire and develop over time, and the ability to connect with your partner. A great sexual connection will not happen by accident. You need to give each other time and attention. The key is not what you do in bed but how you feel about each other.

Toolbox

- Be prepared to meet each other's sexual needs.
- You may not have the same level of desire, but you can understand your partner's needs.
- Don't neglect your sex life or put it last on a long list of things to do.
- Give yourself some uninterrupted time together every week.
- Create an environment, both physically and emotionally, where sex can take place. For example, take a long, hot bath, give each other massages, light candles, play romantic music.
- Take the occasional weekend away, just the two of you.
- Be affectionate to each other. Lots of hugs, kisses and cuddles create an intimate connection.
- Even when you have a young family, create some time alone with your partner.
- Make sure you both retain a sense of humour and have fun as well as sex.

chapter ten

Creating Financial Harmony

WHEN SUE AND PETER MARRIED, she was twenty-eight and he was twenty-five. Sue shares their story.

I was in a well-paid executive position. Peter wanted to start his own business, so I agreed to be the breadwinner until his business was up and running. My family adored Peter. Then we discovered that Peter was gambling, and that he had gone through all our savings. I felt betrayed. My parents were shattered, and terrified for my future. Peter felt bitterly ashamed and unable to face my parents.

We decided to go to Susie for counselling and after the first session we felt hopeful. Susie gave us a practical action plan. She suggested both Peter and my parents start to talk to each other and be civil. She explained that gradual behaviour shifts would change the feelings. This is exactly what happened.

Peter also went for some sessions on his own. Susie helped him to come to terms with the negative experiences in his past and look at his own needs. He felt he had blown his chances by betraying my trust. I was prepared to give him an opportunity to act differently.

We had some setbacks. We would argue and sometimes went for days without speaking to each other. In the beginning, I would want to talk and he would withdraw. Then he would get himself into a hole and he didn't know how to climb out. Susie showed me how to give him a hand to get out of a difficult place.

As the breadwinner, I was also under stress. As Peter had grown up in an environment where he was deprived both emotionally and financially, he was very focused on material things. He wanted to drive an expensive car and live beyond our means. Although I was on a good salary, I drove an older car. He drove a Lexus.

As he overcame his issues, we got rid of his expensive car. We went to therapy once a week for eighteen months, and the results have been wonderful. We now resolve issues more constructively. We have come a long way from those early days when it seemed our marriage would not survive. We have both learnt a lot. Susie encouraged us to treat each other as we would our best friends. Peter has become more flexible and easy-going. He is now the breadwinner while I am at home with the baby. I know he can't wait to get home to us at night.

Even the strongest relationship can be plagued by arguments about money. Couples experience conflict about who earns it, who spends it, how much to save and who manages it.

Financial stress can be destructive to the health and well-being of a relationship. Each partner brings to the relationship their attitude to money, their money personality – whether they are spenders or savers, cautious or risk-takers, and the patterns that they have learnt from their family of origin. In this chapter we explore some constructive and creative ways to deal with money in a relationship. By becoming aware of the role money plays in your relationship, you can avoid many arguments and use money as a tool to achieve your goals.

Do you often find that money is a cause of marital problems?

Yes, finances can play a major role in causing conflict. The range of issues is varied and has changed radically over the past few decades. Women used to marry at around nineteen or twenty. Many women had no job experience, no careers and little formal education. A year after I married I had my first child. I was basically handed over from my parents to my husband. My job was to look after our home. I didn't know anything about how to manage money.

In contrast, many women now marry later, by which time they have studied, established a career and have work experience. Many of them have an opportunity to save before they marry. There are different expectations for the modern couple. Increasingly their earning capacity is considered to be equal, as well as in their roles in the relationship.

Many couples do not discuss financial issues prior to marriage. They spend a lot of time planning the wedding but do not undertake any financial planning. Each partner brings into the marriage their own expectations, acquired from life experience and their family of origin. The differences between the two financial outlooks on life can create major arguments.

Can we look at some of these differences?

In the past, the breadwinner gave his wife a housekeeping allowance. That was the custom when there was only one wage earner. Now many women are working outside the home and finances are handled differently. When couples pay me, they give me joint cheques. I know that joint cheque accounts vary in terms of how they are run but generally it is obvious that women play a much more active role now in managing the family finances.

Some couples have well-thought-out financial structures in place. This is usually when both partners have careers and enjoy financial independence. They work out how much each can contribute to a joint account and how much each is able to keep for their own personal spending. This gives them financial autonomy. One wife who insisted on having a separate account said to me, 'If we had only a joint account and I was to buy my partner a present, I would feel that I was buying it with his money.'

When I was working at a children's hospital as a social worker, I came into contact with many women from socially disadvantaged backgrounds. I remember a few of these women being desperately unhappy in their marriages. They wanted to get out but told me, 'I don't even have the money to buy my baby a bottle of milk, let alone leave the marriage'. They felt trapped financially. Many of them had at least one young child. They were out of the paid workforce and had to ask their partner to give them the money for a pair of stockings or a haircut.

When my son and daughter married, I told both my daughter and daughter-in-law that they should each open an account in their own name; that they should deposit some money in it every week so that they would never feel trapped financially. I have found that women who have some money of their own are more empowered in their relationships. They don't have to ask for every dollar that they want to spend. This gives them financial autonomy and greater self-esteem.

CREATE A SPENDING PLAN

THE HAPPINESS OF YOUR RELATIONSHIP IS MORE IMPORTANT THAN THE AMOUNT OF MONEY YOU HAVE. YOUR METHOD OF MANAGING MONEY AND NEGOTIATING WITH EACH OTHER IS THE FOUNDATION OF FINANCIAL HARMONY. YOUR NEEDS, AND YOUR PARTNER'S, SHOULD BE EQUALLY MET WITH THE AVAILABLE RESOURCES.

I have even seen a number of affluent couples where the wife did not have access to any money. If a woman is not in paid employment and her partner chooses not to give her any money, she could feel just as trapped as a woman from a socially disadvantaged background. With another couple, the wife wanted to refurnish a room in their house. The husband did not see the need for this and he refused to provide the money for her to do it. She was very upset, as she knew he could easily afford to give her the money. After much negotiation in counselling sessions, I finally managed to persuade him to agree to give her some money each month. This was a set amount for her personal use. She could either save up for something she wanted or spend it as she wished. This arrangement worked for her. It made her feel more independent and also taught her how to budget.

This situation can arise at all levels of the income scale. It has more to do with the power balance in the relationship than the amount of money a couple has. Some men with a large earning capacity keep very tight control of their money.

How does it impact the wife if she does not have any say in how the family finances are managed?

It can create dissatisfaction for the wife, especially if she is not earning. If she is a full-time mother and homemaker, the role may be more challenging than a paid job and yet is not rewarded financially.

Many women underestimate their abilities. It is vital that women have access to money even when they are out of the paid workforce in order to maintain their self-esteem and to avoid feeling trapped. A woman needs to know she has a choice; that she can work if she chooses.

What are the benefits for a woman who is financially savvy?

Increasing numbers of women are seeing the importance of becoming knowledgeable about finances. They may learn about the stock market, read the business section of the newspaper and make their own investments. This financial knowledge gives a woman the confidence and information to participate fully in financial decision making.

Isn't it difficult for a woman who has never had to understand or manage the finances to develop her financial knowledge?

At first it may seem very confusing, but like everything else, the more you read and learn, the more you understand. There are also courses at adult education centres that you can attend to increase your knowledge. Women owe it to themselves to develop money management skills. Once women have financial knowledge, they can participate in financial discussions as well as make their own decisions about what to do with their money.

KATHY, AGED THIRTY-NINE, HAS BEEN married to Paul for fifteen years.

One of the things I like about my marriage is that I manage all the finances. My husband has a successful business, but he is an ideas person. He has no interest in budgets, cash flows or money. I know exactly how much money we have, what we can afford, and how we spend our money. I pay all the bills, organise loans, and manage the finances.

Paul is happy with this arrangement as it frees him up to develop his business. I have a deep sense of security in my marriage. I feel empowered and I feel good about myself. I would encourage other women to take an active role in the family finances.

Why is it so important for women to learn about the financial arrangements of their relationship?

Many women outlive their spouses, so not only do they have to cope with the loss of a loved one but they also have to manage the finances of the relationship. No-one can afford to be ignorant of the financial situation of their relationship. It's a reality of life that we all have to deal with. Also, the more knowledge a woman has, the more confidence she has.

I also think it is vital for women bringing up children at home to do some paid work, preferably outside the home. My daughter, who was employed in staff training, gave up her full-time job when her first child was born. She started teaching one night a week at a technical college about six months after her child was born. Fifteen years down the track she is still doing that and much more. It has been a factor contributing to her self-esteem and confidence.

Best of all, she did not have to struggle with re-entering the workforce after a long time away from it. The longer you stay out of your career or the paid workforce, the harder it is to get back into it. Your skills become outdated. You've lost your networks and lost a lot of your confidence. Even if the money you earn is only enough to pay the babysitters, you are at least creating a future path for yourself.

Women who have been long-time homemakers often undervalue their skills. I always encourage them to make a list of all the skills required to run a home efficiently, from dealing with plumbers to looking after children to managing a household budget. Many of these skills should not be undervalued.

LARRY, FORTY-THREE, AND JANE, FORTY-ONE, have been married for a year. Both had been used to a free and easy lifestyle without major responsibilities. Jane is a freelance writer who also teaches English part-time. Larry is a photographer who works from time to time.

Both enjoyed their hippie-style existence and built up no assets. Between them they owned a car, some camera equipment, and Jane's computer. Three months after marrying, Jane was delighted to find herself pregnant. She continued to work part-time until her baby was born. When her baby was six months old, Jane came to see me, feeling very insecure and anxious about their financial situation.

Larry will not take on permanent work. We live from week to week. I get very stressed when I know we don't have sufficient money in our account for next month's rent. With a baby, our bills are higher and I feel very unhappy about our financial situation. I've been breastfeeding, so returning to teaching has not been an option. The hardest thing is that Larry gets upset if I voice my fears. He feels that I undermine him by becoming anxious. He is prepared to borrow money until we are on our feet again. This scares me as I don't want to get into further debt.

Susie suggested we draw up a detailed budget of all our expenses. Then we looked at who would earn the income and who would look after the baby. It was decided that I would work two days a week and Larry would work three days. We were each given responsibility for bringing in a proportion of the income. The days I worked, Larry would take care of the baby, and vice versa.

Each of us would have a certain amount of money each month to use as we wished. This would give us some freedom. Some money would also be directed to a savings account. We had a few follow-up sessions to fine-tune the budget, but once we had a plan, I felt less insecure, and Larry felt less defensive, about our financial situation.

What if you marry someone with a different attitude to money from yours? What if one of you is more extravagant than the other?

Yes, your attitudes to money may be vastly different. One partner may have a strong need for financial security, to save a large proportion of the earnings. The other may want to live as if there is no tomorrow. They may want to borrow money to spend and be more willing to shop on credit. This could be a formula for disaster. You cannot change someone's personality but you can set down some boundaries that you are both comfortable with. You need to find a balance between spending some and saving some and giving some money to charity (if possible). As always, the views of both partners need to be respected. This may require therapy or financial counselling, depending on how far the partners differ in their thinking.

Do you believe budgets are useful?

Budgets are necessary for some couples. It depends on your financial situation.

There are essentials you have to allocate money for, like food and rent. Then there are the 'luxury' categories such as new clothes, and then the special treats like holidays. The first category is non-negotiable. Any leftover money can be divided between the other two categories.

For those who dislike budgeting, another useful tool is to create a spending plan. Collect receipts of all your purchases over a three-month period. Then work out how much you have spent on each category: food, clothes, rent, entertainment and transport. Create a spending plan based on actual expenses and add ten to fifteen per cent to each total. In this way your spending plan may be a more accurate reflection of your spending habits. Budgets are like diets; they make you feel deprived. So save first and design a spending plan that you can afford. It goes without saying that you should always spend less than you earn, otherwise you are continually running into debt. I also find an EFTPOS card is more manageable than a credit card, as you cannot spend money that you do not have.

That's right. Also, for people who have difficulty managing their spending, it is advisable for them to decide in advance how much they want to spend each week and draw that specific amount of cash out of the bank. In this way they can see when their money is running out.

If you find it difficult to save, arrange an automatic transfer into a savings account at the beginning of the month, or when you get paid. If you save before you spend, you will not miss the money you have put aside and it feels like a bonus when you see it building up in your savings account.

A couple needs to address their financial situation both before they marry and then again at various times, especially when they go through periods of change. This may include the birth of a baby, changing jobs, one partner deciding to study, buying a property or any other major purchase.

Another good practice is to have a regular money talk where you sit down quietly together with a notebook and calculator and write down your financial goals, your spending and saving plans. I believe you need to evaluate this plan on a regular basis to accommodate changes and see if it is working. You need to discuss with your partner who is going to manage the finances, bills and payments on a monthly basis.

Another important area you need to discuss and share is the making of financial decisions. Sharing information about money is an essential part of your communication pattern. You both have to decide how much detail is relevant in your situation.

It is important not to have one partner controlling everything, with the other person in the dark. There are times where one partner is not interested in participating. It is often the woman. I believe that women create a vulnerable position for themselves by not being involved. Joint financial decisions, sharing financial information and setting mutually acceptable financial goals are an essential part of any relationship. Often financial decisions are based on the values that a couple holds. To clarify how money is spent, a couple needs to define their values.

I agree. Start having healthy financial discussions early on in the relationship. There can be a lot of secrecy around money. Make sure you get the subject out into the open and discuss the issues. This is far less expensive than going to court! Take care before you sign documents. Don't sign any that guarantee your partner's business debts or car loans. Many partners have been left legally responsible for their partner's debts when the relationship ended. The fiercest arguments around money arise at the time of divorce and separation. It has been said we marry for love but when we part, money becomes the central issue. If you find that you and your partner cannot sit down calmly to discuss financial arrangements, use the services of a mediator.

Toolbox

- Be prepared to discuss financial issues before you marry and then regularly once you are married.
- Discuss the roles you will each play in the relationship. Will you both work full-time, part-time, or will only one of you work? What about the unpaid work in the home and looking after the children?
- Who will manage the household budget? Pay the bills?
- Will you have a joint account or will you each have your own account? Possibly you may have a joint account for household expenses.
- Accept that your partner may have experienced different ways of managing money from you.
- Your partner may have a different money personality from you. One of you may enjoy spending, the other saving. One of you may be cautious; the other prepared to take risks. Discuss and find compromises you can both live with.
- You should each have some money each month to spend as you please. The amount obviously depends on your financial circumstances.
- Both partners should have all relevant information about their finances.

chapter eleven

How to Decide if it's Really Over

ANNE IS A THIRTY-NINE-YEAR-OLD WITH two sons, aged eight and ten, and works full-time as a sales representative. Two years ago, her husband was offered an executive position in London. Her husband wanted the family to follow him. Anne was faced with a dilemma.

I had already spent time living overseas when my husband was studying. I knew what the move would entail. At home we had friends and family, the children were settled, and I had my job. To live abroad I would have to give up all the things that meant a lot to me. I realised that we wanted different things. I had to ask myself whether I loved my husband enough to uproot myself and the children. I realised my love was not strong enough to withstand another major upheaval.

Had we not been faced with this dilemma, our marriage may have drifted on. I went through a period of indecisiveness. Should I do it out of duty? Should I do it for the sake of my children? Is this my lot in life? I went for counselling and came to the realisation that I do not have to keep giving in to my husband's demands. I decided to stay with my sons. He went.

Eighteen months later he changed jobs again, this time going to Singapore. I was so relieved we had stayed put. We are now divorced, I'm in a new relationship, and have found what I'm looking for. There were many painful moments, but the most challenging part was making the decision. My advice to other women is to clarify what you want for yourself, be prepared to take on extra responsibilities, and don't stay in a relationship for the wrong reasons.

What are some of the signs that a relationship is in danger?

One of the signs is that there is little communication. Another sign is when a couple no longer enjoys each other's company and may not even like each other any more. They may have drifted apart and no longer have anything in common. It's all very well to have independence, but we also need to have togetherness.

One of the partners may stop feeling loved, nurtured, respected or appreciated. A lack of interest in maintaining the sexual relationship can also be an indicator of problems in the marriage. Another clear symptom of a serious problem is when one or both partners are having an affair. This is a sign that they need to go outside the marriage to have their needs met, rather than confronting the issues in the relationship.

For some couples who have always spoken to each other with respect, a change in the pattern of communication could indicate stress in the relationship. They may shout at each other and become verbally abusive. These are signs that there is anger, pain and frustration. If a couple already has a volatile relationship, there is a much greater risk of emotional or physical abuse when the stress increases.

Another reason that communication breaks down is that there are too many 'taboo' subjects. If you continually avoid bringing up difficult subjects in case your partner becomes upset, the issues remain unresolved and seething below the surface. This can cause great resentment. Try to deal with problems as and when they arise and they will usually be more manageable.

When should you see a therapist?

The sooner you go, the easier it is to resolve the problem. It's much harder if you wait until the relationship is on the verge of collapse. I have some couples who continue to come to see me every six months. There are no couples who don't ever have any issues. Usually they can be resolved without therapy, but if not, a couple should have counselling before giving up on the marriage.

When is it destructive to stay in a relationship?

Definitely when there is physical abuse. I believe that if children are exposed to verbal, emotional or physical abuse it is likely that they perceive that behaviour as a way to deal with hurt, anger and conflict. That is what they will reproduce in their own relationships. If you do not want your child to duplicate abusive behaviour, fix it or get out. I have treated several men who have been physically abusive, but with therapy and at times with the help of medication, they have learnt to express their anger and aggression in a more constructive way.

You mentioned that you went through a divorce. How were you able to model a happy relationship for your children?

I divorced my first husband when my children were nine and ten years old. I was a single mother for ten years. During this time, my children did not have the role model of a happy relationship. I married my second husband a few years before my daughter married.

In the speech I made at her wedding, I said how grateful I was that my daughter had the opportunity to observe a relationship that contained love, mutual respect, warmth, caring, laughter, common interests and good communication. These were all the wonderful things I wanted her to experience. By witnessing my present marriage close at hand for two years prior to her own marriage, she was able to model this behaviour in her own relationship.

How can we deal with pain in a positive way?

In every marriage there is pain and conflict. What is important is to resolve that pain. It is vital that children learn how to deal with anger in a constructive way. From the moment children are brought into a relationship, parents have an obligation to remember that they are role models.

I tell my clients, 'Try hard to treat each other with respect, even when you are in the process of separation'. In my opinion, separation counselling should be compulsory. The pain experienced by the couple is often so great that they express it in destructive ways. We may become irrational, impulsive, and desire to hurt the other person. When there are children present it is always they who pay the price. Also, in a subconscious way we want our children to side with us. We may share our feelings with our children, and they struggle to cope with this in their desire to remain loyal to both parents.

So when do you call it quits? When do you say, 'Enough is enough, I'm leaving'?

Every situation is different. There is no formula dictating when couples should separate. The dying stages of a relationship may have very different faces. It may be continual fighting, arguing and shouting. On the other hand, there may be nothing left to say and that silence can be deafening. It may be an indication that one or both parties don't care any more. They may be tired of fighting. They may not like each other any longer.

You have to ask yourself some tough questions. I ask couples, 'Is there something left? What was it like when you first got together? Did you laugh, have fun, joke and enjoy each other's company? What happened to change that dynamic? What do you fight about? Do you have the motivation to resolve the issues that are killing your love and respect for each other? Is the marriage worth saving?'

Why do couples often fight about such trivial things?

Sometimes we fight and bicker about trivial things to avoid dealing with a deeper problem. The real issue at stake may be too frightening to confront. You need to ask yourself what is the underlying issue that is causing the pain. Have the courage to dig deeper; once you have worked on the important problem, the trivial matters will dissolve.

It seems obvious to try to meet your partner's needs, yet it's not always easy to when you are struggling yourself.

Exactly. We are not taught how to be married or live together. We start off happy, connected and willing to please each other. Gradually we start to destroy our relationships. If we turn away from our partner and refuse to satisfy his needs, we are choosing to weaken our relationship. If we accept this behaviour from our partner, we are playing the victim, putting up with less and less nurturing. Try to look beyond the surface. Why is your partner afraid to give you emotional comfort? What does he feel?

Women seem to have a greater need for closeness and intimacy than men. How do we reconcile this difference?

Another cause of friction may be the husband spending a lot of time working so that he has no quality time with the family. For him, providing for the family may be an important value priority, but the wife may gladly give up some luxuries in order to have her husband spend more time with her and their children. This situation requires negotiation. Often there is no right or wrong. If values conflict, work through these and find a solution that is acceptable to both parties. If not, arguments will continue. The couple may stop arguing about the real issues but resentment will emerge in unrelated issues.

It is vital to establish your priorities. A husband may want time to play football and see his mates, feeling that he is entitled to have some leisure time since his wife is at home all day. His wife may feel he should be involved in family activities in his leisure time. A compromise is needed so that both partners feel their needs are being met. There is no point in one person giving up on what he needs to satisfy the other, and then feeling resentful.

What advice do you give when one partner is having an affair?
In most marriages there is an unspoken agreement about fidelity, so that they sometimes fall apart if a third party becomes involved. When I speak to each partner on their own, I ask them if there is another person involved. If the couple wants to save their marriage I refuse to work with them unless the affair is over or put on hold. You cannot have your needs met elsewhere and expect be able to work on your marriage. Some couples have an open marriage where they can accept their partner having an affair and stay together. This only works if both partners feel comfortable with this situation.

WHEN IN DOUBT, DON'T

IF YOU CAN'T MAKE UP YOUR MIND ABOUT A TOUGH SITUATION, WAIT UNTIL YOU CAN. DON'T MAKE A DECISION UNTIL YOU FEEL CERTAIN YOU'RE MAKING THE RIGHT ONE FOR YOU. TRUST YOUR INSTINCTS.

Are there situations where getting out is the better option?
Alcohol is a cause of relationship breakdown that is hard to resolve. I counselled one couple where the husband would walk in the door every night after work armed with a six-pack and drink himself into a stupor. He would then become aggressive and verbally abusive.

His wife was suffering terribly. She said, 'I have low self-esteem, I feel I've lost my dignity, my pride and my identity'. She felt that by staying in the relationship she was giving him the message that she was willing to put up with his drinking. She gave him an ultimatum. 'Give up drinking, get professional help, or I'll leave'. He was unsuccessful in controlling his drinking problem and his wife decided to leave the marriage.

Both partners need to take responsibility for the situation. Blaming each other will not solve any problems. Ask yourself, 'What have I contributed to the situation? Is he drinking because I cannot meet his needs? How can I support him?' Staying, and allowing the alcoholic to continue drinking, is destructive to your emotional health as well as your children's well-being. Before you end the relationship, whatever the problem is, ask yourself the following tough questions:

- What were the qualities that attracted you to your partner in the first place?
- What do you want and need from a relationship?
- Do you want to stay married, regardless of the quality of the marriage?
- Have you lost your pride, dignity and self-respect by staying?
- What is the price of leaving?
- What are you personally doing to destroy the relationship?
- What are your fears about leaving?
- What do you risk by staying?
- How will you manage financially?

LIZ shares her story:

I know from my own personal experience that the decision is the hardest part. Before I divorced, I spent months vacillating. One day I would wake and think, 'I'm definitely leaving'. The next day I would think, 'It's not so terrible, I could tolerate this for a bit longer'. Eventually with the help of some confronting therapy, supportive friends and a clear belief that I deserved happiness, I made the decision to leave. You have to understand that while leaving may bear a material cost, financial insecurity, social upheaval and considerable pain, staying may be even more damaging. But the period of decision making is fraught with fears, insecurities and pain for both parties.'

Do you separate first or just plan to divorce? Is there a best way?

The act of separation is very serious and is usually the first stage of divorce. Some couples have a very volatile relationship and they go though the process of breaking up and getting back together over and over again. This can be destructive, especially when children are involved. Each time parents get back together, children are filled with hope. Then their hopes are dashed when it falls apart again. I believe it is more beneficial to stay together, have counselling or therapy and only make the decision to separate when you are certain that it is your chosen course of action.

What is the purpose of therapy during the separation process?

When a marriage dies, you also experience the death of the hopes and dreams you shared with your partner. It is better not to have the regret that you did not try everything before taking that final step. Don't leave any stone unturned, otherwise the fear that you did not do enough will come back to haunt you. At least if you go for help you can say, 'We went for help and it was beyond help'. You can choose to have a period of separation before you make the final decision. You need to have therapy in this time. Otherwise you are apart and don't necessarily learn to deal any more effectively with each other. You may miss each other, but once you come back together, the old unresolved issues will still be there.

I also fight for the emotional health and well-being of the children. I come down heavily on mothers and fathers. I always tell separating parents to never say anything derogatory about each other to their children. When you throw an arrow at your partner in the presence of your children, that arrow lodges in the heart of your child. That person will always be your child's mother or father. The child feels great loyalty to both parents.

I was always aware that when I reminded my children to write to their father, ring him on his birthday, make him a card for Father's Day or buy him a gift, I was teaching them how to treat a parent. If that's how they should treat the person I divorced, surely I was teaching them how to treat me.

At what point does the separation become divorce?

When either party is certain that the marriage is not worth saving. There are a number of stages that lead to divorce and some of these processes take place before the physical event occurs. Once the decision has been made by one or both parties, therapy is essential. Getting support through the dark days can help in many ways, and hopefully it can help you make decisions and cope with the difficult times.

What if you can't afford to leave as you have no money of your own?

One thing I encourage women to do, especially those who have been married and out of the workforce for a long time, is some financial planning. Apart from the fact that many women are prevented from leaving a bad marriage by the lack of money, I believe every woman should have some of her own money just in case. Everyone should have an untouchable account so that if you find yourself in an unbearable relationship you can afford to leave. Whatever your level of income, put some money away every week. This provides a woman with some security should things go wrong in her relationship.

There is often a gap between the time you separate and when the financial settlement is made. When the relationship is acrimonious, you could find yourself cut off without funds. With some money behind you, you would be less likely to accept being treated in an unreasonable manner. This is especially relevant in an abusive relationship, because a woman may see no way out financially. From the first time you start feeling that you cannot continue in the marriage, start saving as much as you can. If you think the bank account may be discovered, put the money in a safe-deposit box or ask someone you trust to keep it for you. It may seem devious, but it is very important to safeguard your future.

Some couples stay in the same house after they separate. What are your views on this arrangement?

Living together once you have both decided the marriage is over can be a very painful and destructive process. Some couples do it as an interim phase until one partner can move out. Lack of adequate finances is often behind such a decision. This is another reason why it is important to have some of your own independent resources

Another important thing for both parties to do is to each see their own solicitor to find out what your rights are. Get professional advice; don't rely on your friends. Each person's situation is different. A useful task to perform before you go to a solicitor is to prepare a detailed history of your family finances. This makes your solicitor's task much easier and will in turn save you money.

What is the best way to tell the children about the separation?

Plan when and how you are going to tell the children. First work out with your partner what the living arrangements will be and then explain the situation to the children. Don't burden them with the responsibility of making choices at this point. Change as little as is humanly possible. Try to keep them in the same neighbourhood, at the same school, and retain as much of their routine as you can. The less you change the better, at such a shattering time for them. Much depends on the age of the children as to how much you tell them. Discuss this with a therapist and try not to use the children as a foil in your conflict with your partner.

Don't deprive your children of love, and don't let your anger at your partner deprive them of love from his extended family. If your children have a good relationship with your partner's family, keep that connection. You are not divorcing your partner's family. When I got divorced I went to my in-laws to tell them that they would continue to play an important role in my children's lives, and I made sure that the children saw both sets of grandparents on a regular basis.

As far as your partner is concerned, just remember that even though you are getting divorced, you will have to work together to parent the children, if they are very young, for a long time to come. So developing reasonable channels of communication is an important part of getting divorced if you have children.

What you are saying is logical but not easy, as often the reason for getting divorced is lack of positive communication.

That's why I think therapeutic support and counselling while you are in the process of separation and divorce is important. Even if your communication skills have been poor, it's never too late to learn. It is especially necessary at this time, as both partners will experience a lot of anger. A therapist will help you deal with this.

What about the social side? How do you deal with friends, especially shared friends?

Friends do not have to take sides. Tell your friends they do not have to be the meat in the sandwich or the go-between. Apart from a few very close friends with whom I bared my soul and shared my tears, I put on a good front to everyone else. Even if your partner is criticising you, don't lower yourself to that level. You will gain the respect of all your friends by refraining. They will think less of your partner for running you down.

Never lower yourself to someone else's standards. Maintain your dignity. That person is your child's parent and always will be. Divorce therapy helps minimise the negative effects on your children while getting support for you. Your children will cope the way you cope.

You should expect your social life to change when you go through a divorce. It takes a while for friendships to settle down again. Concentrate on a few friends who give you trust, love and support. Expect to go through a few months when you feel as if you are on an emotional seesaw. One day you feel up, another day it all feels overwhelming. Expect these emotions and find ways to deal with your grief and pain. Some people cope by taking up exercise, others start meditation and yoga or other activity that helps fill the void and relieve the painful emotions.

There will be times when you start to question whether you were right to leave the relationship. Most people who go through divorce have experienced times when they cannot remember what it was that made them so miserable in the marriage. For this reason, I strongly advise people to make a list of all the factors that contributed to the break up of the relationship. It is best to do this as soon as possible after the separation. Note all the problems you had: the arguments, the lack of shared interests, the lack of love, affection, respect or sex, and any form of abuse. If you didn't argue, did either of you withdraw from the relationship to the extent that the silences were deafening? These reasons or others contributed to the unhappiness in your marriage. In moments of sadness and self-doubt about whether you made the right decision, you can remind yourself how miserable you were and that you deserve to be happy. Now write down what action you can take to plan a happier future. If you cannot do it alone, enlist the help of a therapist.

Toolbox

- If there is verbal, physical or sexual abuse in your relationship, seriously consider getting professional counselling.
- Having an affair will put your relationship at risk, as it will destroy trust. Decide if this is worth it.
- If you are having an affair, you should put it on hold until you have decided whether you are staying or leaving your relationship.
- Think back to why you married your partner in the first place. Do any of those feelings still exist?
- Do you want to stay married, regardless of the quality of the relationship?
- What are you doing to destroy the marriage? What is your role in it?
- What do you need from a relationship?
- Is there a way of you getting your needs met in this relationship?
- Have you explored all avenues to try to stay together and work on the relationship?
- If you do decide to split up, get counselling during the process.
- Your children will cope the way you cope.

chapter twelve

Divorce and Repartnering Without Destruction

VANESSA, FORTY, AND DEAN, FORTY-TWO, had been married for seventeen years and had two children, Mandy, thirteen, and Benjamin, eleven. Vanessa and Dean had spent the last two years either arguing or withdrawing from each other.

There was no warmth, and no friendship or mutual interests; they had grown too far apart. They were also experiencing financial problems. Dean was working very long hours, and Vanessa was feeling totally neglected by him. The problem they approached me with was that the children were answering back, their marks at school were deteriorating, and Vanessa had been called into school after Mandy had been rude to the teachers.

By the end of our first session, it became evident that the underlying problem to the children's misbehaviour was the marital strife that the children were exposed to at home. We worked on trying to improve the marriage, but after two months, Vanessa decided that she wanted a divorce. Dean was devastated, but for Vanessa it was the only option. She felt that divorce was better for the children than growing up with parents in an unhappy marriage.

With divorce seeming the only option, our next aim was to ensure the divorce was as amicable as possible, for their sake and for the sake of the children. So Vanessa and Dean developed, and agreed to, a set of rules. To minimise the harmful effects of divorce on the children, ongoing therapy and enormous effort on their part was needed. After a few months, the divorce was finalised amicably. Both Vanessa and Dean felt the therapy had been worthwhile, especially for the sake of the children.

Despite the fact that the divorce rate is still increasing and couples of all ages are ending their long-term commitments, nothing diminishes the pain, destruction and trauma of this event. Knowing so many other people get divorced does not make the process any easier for the individual going through it.

For some, the sense of loss is even greater than if the person had been bereaved. It is the death of a marriage, the death of dreams and for many, a loss of self and identity. This loss may vary, depending on the length of the marriage, how dependent the person was on the relationship and how much energy she had invested in her partner.

If children are involved, this means there is an ongoing connection with each other after the divorce. Starting over is not easy and the emotional journey is different for men and women, depending on the extent of change required in their lifestyle and circumstances. There may be feelings of guilt, failure and betrayal as well as financial, physical and lifestyle changes. We will initially look at divorce from a woman's perspective and then examine the experience of men.

What are some of the feelings women experience after divorce?

One of my clients, Linda, is recently emerging from a traumatic break-up. She told me:

I fell into an abyss. I was overwhelmed with fear and confusion. I couldn't eat, I couldn't sleep, and I was left in a shambles financially. I had spent fifteen years looking after my husband's needs and his happiness, trying to become the person he wanted me to be. We looked like the perfect family but I was dying inside. When my third child was diagnosed with severe learning disorders, my partner gave me very little support. That was the beginning of the end. I cried all the time. I had been out of the workforce for twelve years, from the time my first child was born. I had lost confidence in myself and in my abilities. I almost hit rock bottom.

Then I joined a support group for newly divorced women. I found a place where I could express my feelings. It was a place where I could cry and also be heard. There was also the reassurance that other women had reached rock bottom but come through.

I found one-on-one counselling to be very helpful. I went through the painful process of putting myself back together again. I think it takes about two years after divorce to work through the grieving process and come back to the person you really are. You are different at the end of the journey.

ANOTHER CLIENT, JULIE, whose husband left her for another woman after eighteen years, said:

I felt as if I was having a bad dream, floating around, lost. I had that stunned feeling. I would cry all day. I felt like a failure and I began to doubt myself as a mother. Now, five years later, I can't believe how far I've come. After totally falling apart, I went back to college and retrained as a bookkeeper. I lecture twice a week at a business college, and have my own consultancy doing bookkeeping and accounting for small businesses.

I bought myself a small cottage after we sold our family home. I joined the gym, changed my hairstyle, lost weight and now feel much better about myself. Part of the pain was saying goodbye to the perfect picture of a happy marriage. It was a myth, as my husband was cheating on me. It was farewell to a life that was comfortable and predictable.

What are some of the steps women can take at this stage to move forward?

I encourage couples to have therapy during separation and divorce but also afterwards, if they need it. If you don't connect with the first therapist you see, keep trying until you find one you feel comfortable with. Someone who is caring, unbiased, and who will listen to both partners equally. The aim of therapy is not to find out who is right and who is wrong, who is the victim and who is the villain. When both partners are hurting, the aim is to minimise any further pain. I like to see the couple together but sometimes one partner may need ongoing individual therapy.

For a woman who has concentrated on the role of wife and mother during her marriage, half of her identity is lost when the marriage breaks up and she may well feel devastated. After allowing herself an initial period of about two to three months to digest the loss, I would encourage her to start planning her life as a single person. Much will depend on finances. For most women, getting paid employment will be a priority. They may need to requalify, study further or do something creative. My friends also encouraged me to use make-up, get a new haircut and wear contact lenses instead of glasses. It is vital to make the most of yourself so that you feel better about yourself and so rebuild your confidence.

KEEP ARGUMENTS TO A MINIMUM

DON'T MAKE A BIG ISSUE OUT OF EVERY DISAGREEMENT. NOT ALL PROBLEMS ARE SOLVABLE. THERE ARE TIMES WHERE YOU HAVE TO AGREE TO DISAGREE. ASK YOURSELF, 'IS THIS WORTH AN ARGUMENT?'

When I got divorced thirty years ago, divorce was not as prevalent as it is today. I was thirty-one and I had two children, aged nine and ten. I had had no education after high school and

I knew that I had to equip myself to earn a living and provide for my children. I went back to university and studied Social Work for six years part-time. I was fortunate to have my parents helping me financially while I was studying. It was the best thing I could have done, as I had no time to wallow in self-pity. My ex-husband did not spend much time with the children so I had almost full-time responsibilities for childcare as well as having to provide financially.

I started seeing other men shortly after my divorce. I was still young and I was keen to have a life. It was also important for me to see myself and my children as a whole family, not a broken family, so I concentrated on creating a happy home atmosphere so that the children could invite their friends around. It also helped that my ex-husband and I never said negative things about each other to anyone. He encouraged the children to respect me and they were encouraged to see him.

Another thing that a woman often experiences after divorce is social isolation. Many of her female friends may feel threatened, fearing that their husbands will find the newly divorced friend attractive. I remember one of my friend's husbands making an overture to me and it was very tempting to respond to his attention. I'm glad my loyalty to my friend was strong enough to enable me to resist him. It was hard enough coping with all the other aspects of divorce.

This attitude resulted in me being no threat to my female friends. I also decided early on that I would put on a happy face when I was out socially. I found myself always surrounded by a large group of old and new friends I had a few close friends with whom I could share my tears and express my feelings. Apart from them, I put a smile on my face and was determined to be positive.

Age is a worry for many older divorced women. Some women ask me, 'Am I too old to start again?' If they have decided to divorce, I assure them that whatever their age, it's their attitude that is critical. One of the things I encourage women to do is forgive themselves. Forgive yourself for any mistakes you may have made. We can dwell on the past and drive ourselves mad, or we can forgive ourselves and move on.

How long should you wait before you start dating or seeing other men?

Opinions vary on as to how long to wait before you start dating. I was introduced to a young doctor a week after separation, much to the shock of some of my friends. After a few weeks, I invited him to escort me to a dinner party. It was practically unheard of in my community to even have a divorce back in 1968.

I also made it clear to my friends that they didn't have to choose who they wanted to be friends with. If my ex-husband and I bumped into each other we were friendly, although however amicable the divorce has been, seeing your partner with another partner is always difficult. Be prepared for when it happens. Starting a new relationship depends on your particular circumstances, your age, how bruised you are, and whether you feel ready to meet new people. If you feel very vulnerable you may not feel like presenting yourself. When you do start meeting men and dating, don't spend the evening talking about the drama of your divorce or your ex-husband. I remember thinking I did not want to date men who had been single for less than one year. I did not want to act as someone's therapist on a date!

What about men? Do they experience similar emotions of loss, identity crisis and pain?

It depends on who leaves and who is left. When men leave, it's quite often for someone else who is already lined up. When a man has been left or asked to leave, he has to find a place to live, and he may need to learn domestic skills such as cooking, cleaning and doing laundry. He may also be in shock, not having realised that his relationship was in trouble.

Men often react with anger, which lingers for a long while unless they get help in dealing with these strong emotions. Some men may become violent, emotionally volatile, even dangerous. Some women may also experience extreme anger and feel tempted to vandalise their husband's car or something equally precious to him. This sort of behaviour is unacceptable and only results in exacerbating the conflict. It can often be precipitated by feelings of loss and abandonment. Some men miss their children very much if they have limited access or if they do not spend much time with them. They also miss the comfort of their home and family life. When the situation is not of their choosing, this can generate feelings of rage and frustration. Some men try to get back at wives who have left them by withholding maintenance and using money as a weapon, or embark on numerous sexual encounters as a way of salvaging their wounded egos.

Another major problem for men to handle is finances. When a man first separates he may find himself running two homes. He has to pay two lots of rent and food, and his expenses increase drastically. He may experience extreme financial pressure which will add to his pain, isolation and anger.

What can they do to help themselves?

Like women, men can join a support group where they can connect with men going through similar experiences. They can also have individual therapy to help them make sense of what has happened in their life. I also encourage men to have a physical outlet in sport: running, working out at the gym, boxing or swimming. I recommend any activity that will reduce the stress and create a feeling of well-being.

Many men would benefit from counselling after separation, to help them deal with the issues that arise from the divorce, such as access, maintenance and the financial settlement.

How do both men and women go about meeting a new partner?
Introductions through friends or work are a good way. Also, it is worth considering going to an introductions agency or advertising. One of my clients recently met a man through an ad in a newspaper and they are incredibly happy.

I know of a woman who just married and she met her partner on the Internet. I guess you need to be open to opportunities and creative. Do you have any advice for when starting to date again?
Once you do meet someone new, I would not rush into any aspect of the relationship. I would not introduce children to a new partner until you have seen him/her a few times. When you do, it may be best not to express affection in front of the children too soon. If you separated as the result of an affair, I would not publicly date that person until a few weeks have passed. Also, resist baring your soul to a stranger; take it slowly at the beginning so that you can build up trust. Don't go into every date thinking that this is Mr/Ms Right. Instead, focus on having an enjoyable evening. Be yourself and relax.

When starting a new relationship, take care that you understand why your marriage came unstuck. Both partners need to take responsibility for the marriage breakdown. The crucial thing is not to repeat the same mistakes with a second partner. Self-awareness, understanding the issues, and healing from the pain and hurt of the separation/divorce are prerequisites to moving on to a new partner.

When is it acceptable to move in with a new partner?
Don't rush into moving in with a new partner. Allow the relationship to grow slowly. Gradually introduce the children into the situation and allow time for new bonds to form. Second-time round can be wonderful, but it can also be complicated by having to deal with stepchildren and blended families.

What are some of the issues we should consider before marrying again?

It is vital that negative feelings left over from a first marriage and divorce are resolved before you embark on a second marriage. Coming to terms with divorce involves an understanding of why the marriage broke down. Both partners need to acknowledge the role they played in the process. They need to go through the sadness, grief, guilt and anger associated with the divorce.

When these emotions have been faced and expressed, a person is more likely to be ready for a new relationship. There is so much disappointment and sadness in ending a marriage. Both partners need time to come to terms with these feelings. It is important to gain clarity and insight into why the first relationship ended, so that you do not repeat the same mistakes.

How can we achieve this insight?

If you are confused about why your first marriage ended then counselling may be helpful to you. It is challenging to end one marriage but even more distressing to have a subsequent relationship end. Invest in yourself. Learn to understand yourself and what you need. You may make these discoveries alone, through talking to friends, or you may choose to see a professional.

How can we understand what we need second time around?

Think about your priorities and what your needs are. You are likely to be at a different stage in your life from when you married the first time. A second marriage will be a different relationship from a first marriage. You may be more independent, already have children from a first marriage and want companionship, intimacy and emotional security.

You also need to look at your patterns for resolving conflict and ensure that you have the tools to sort out problems. Make a list of all the issues that came up for you with your first partner. Are any of the past patterns repeating themselves? Sometimes we unconsciously choose the same kind of person as we did the first time around.

If you are not sure whether the new relationship is right for you, you could ask yourself the following questions:

- Do I feel happy and relaxed with my new partner?
- Do I feel I can talk about any issue to him?
- Do I feel my partner likes my children?
- Am I sexually compatible with my partner?
- Do I share the same values?
- Do I have some similar interests?
- Do I like my new partner's children and extended family?
- Can I maintain the lifestyle I have created for myself?

Is there anything else we should consider?

Finances are a more complex issue the second time around. If you have been single for a long time between relationships you may have become used to making your own financial decisions. Work out who will pay for what; be clear about obligations to children and ex-spouses.

You may want to draw up a pre-nuptial contract so that you can each protect your assets. Clarify whether you will have a joint account or separate bank accounts. Think carefully about the level of financial involvement you want to have in the new relationship. Whose house will you live in, or will you buy a new home together?

Some of your feelings about finances may be a residue from the settlement of your first marriage. If you feel that you were disadvantaged in the settlement, you may be reluctant to share your financial resources with your new partner. A gradual combining of finances can often be the answer.

Whose house should you live in?

There is no cut and dried answer to this, as situations differ. One partner may have custody of the children and not want to move them from their familiar surroundings. Another partner may need a bigger house so that both sets of children can be accommodated.

Houses tend to symbolise more than just a place to live. You may not feel comfortable living in a house that previously belonged to the first spouse and vice versa. Often a new home, neutral territory, may be the best choice.

That sounds like a good idea. We did that when I remarried. However, I still felt sad selling the unit I had purchased for myself. It represented my independence. But we needed a home large enough to accommodate both sets of children.

What about the roles we play in the new relationship? If you are about to remarry, it is wise to discuss the expectations that you both have with regards to the household tasks, and the roles you will play in the new family. Will you both work? Will one of you work part-time? Who will shop, cook, clean and ferry the kids around?

Especially when children are younger, it is useful to think carefully about what kind of care and support they need and who will provide it. You may like things done in a traditional way and your partner may like a more flexible arrangement or vice versa. Discuss, brainstorm and negotiate possible variations.

How do we talk to our children about remarriage?

Give your children advance warning of the impending event. Let them get to know your prospective partner as well as possible and explain how you feel about him. Your marriage symbolises the real end to the original family. Expect that they may have some difficult feelings and support them.

Toolbox

- Divorce is a very traumatic event. The longer you have been married, the greater the sense of loss. You may experience a huge identity crisis.
- Another factor that may impact on feelings is when one person leaves unexpectedly. The other partner then has shock to deal with also.
- If there another party involved, the other partner has to deal with betrayal as well as loss.
- Make sure that the person you are involved with does not have the same personality characteristics as you ex-partner.
- Do you understand why you first marriage failed? What was your role in its demise?
- Divorce can be filled with rage and anger. Make sure you have some support systems in place.
- Don't ever make your child feel guilty for loving their other parent.
- Before you marry or move in with a new partner, discuss how finances will be handled and who will be responsible for various expenses.
- Make sure you take the children's feelings into account when you repartner. If your children are at a vulnerable age, for example, in their early teens, they may be resistant to your new partner.

section three

Parenting

Parenting is the most important job that any person will undertake, yet most of us are unprepared for this task – unfortunately, children don't come into the world with instructions! During my fourteen years as a private therapist, many clients have come to me with the same question: 'How can I get my children to do as they are told?' Parents often find themselves in a challenging role for which they have no training. To make matters worse, every time they read a book on parenting, the 'experts' seem to contradict each other.

As parents, we shape the life of an individual and create an emotional environment where the child can develop his potential. Most of us have an abundance of love and goodwill, but we also need specific strategies to help us parent well.

We will make you aware at each stage of a child's upbringing how you can enhance a child's self-worth, and develop open and constructive communication. It is vital to be consistent from the cradle onwards. It is much more difficult to remedy bad parenting habits later.

We also look at the impact of divorce and separation on a child's emotional development and provide guidelines to minimise the harmful effects of this potentially traumatic experience. We also lead you through from birth and the toddler phase to primary school and the challenges of adolescence. At each stage we provide case studies to illustrate how others may have dealt with similar issues and practical tools to work issues out for yourself. You will be able to apply this insight to your own situation. The advice is always practical and easy to implement.

The two common factors that emerge in all the chapters are self-esteem and communication skills. We need to learn how to teach our children healthy communication patterns so that they carry these practices into adulthood.

We find ourselves coming full circle. Effective communication enables us to form healthy relationships not only with our partners but also with our children, friends, work colleagues and the world at large.

chapter thirteen

Coping with a New Arrival

Linda and Stephen had problems coping with their six-week old baby boy, Jason. He cried a lot during the day and woke frequently at night. Linda was concerned that the baby was not settled enough to eat, but the reason for him being unsettled was actually that he was hungry. Linda was too exhausted to feed Jason as often as he needed, and Jason was not gaining as much weight as they had hoped he would.

After discussing various alternatives with Susie, Stephen and I decided to offer Jason the bottle after the night feed. Stephen said he wanted to feed the baby the bottle because he had noticed that feeding was such a bonding experience for me.

Once the baby was drinking happily from the bottle and was much more settled, Stephen suggested that he give Jason a bottle at the early morning feed. This gave Linda a chance to catch up on some sleep. It also allowed Stephen to take responsibility for Jason. Linda and Stephen found an added benefit. On their wedding anniversary, they were able to happily leave Jason with Linda's mother while they went out to celebrate, knowing Grandma could give the baby a bottle.

People look forward to the arrival of a baby, hardly anticipating the stresses that accompany this special time. They imagine it will be a time of sheer joy. They put a lot of time into planning the baby's room and into purchasing all the equipment they will need, but do not anticipate the impact the baby will have on their relationship.

Many mothers experience a great shock when they take their first baby home from hospital. They expect to bond with the baby as soon as it is born, but this does not always happen.

Susie, what has your experience in this area revealed?
When I was working at Tresillian, I ran a support group for new mothers. The differences between mothers and their ability to bond with their new babies were extreme. One mother's eyes glowed when she spoke about the love that welled up inside her from the moment her baby was born. Another mother in the group said she felt guilty hearing this because she was feeling little connection to her baby. A number of factors were contributing to her feelings. Her marriage was going through a difficult patch, she had wanted a girl, not a boy, and the baby was unattractive and blotchy.

What can we do to prepare ourselves for parenthood?
Have discussions with your partner about your financial situation. Discuss the pros and cons of you staying at home to take care of the baby, or resuming work. Create a financial plan to cope with the time you are at home with the baby.

Once you make a decision to have a baby, expect dramatic changes after the birth. Expect that you will feel tired and that your relationship will undergo changes. You will not have as much time alone with your partner, your freedom will be diminished and for some there is a loss of identity. You may feel lonely and isolated. To counteract this, keep in touch with your friends and work networks. When the baby is a few months old, reconnect with work colleagues and move out of an 'all baby' environment.

Having a baby can be the most exciting, positive experience for a couple if they prepare for it. Nurture the emotional stability of your relationship with your partner. This strength will help you overcome many of the hurdles of the early stages of caring for a baby. Try to find creative solutions to problems as they arise. Take one day at a time. In the long run, the pleasure that children bring far outweighs the early difficulties.

How does a new baby impact on a woman's life?

One of the amazing things I discovered was that professional women such as solicitors, accountants and high-powered executives often found it extremely difficult to adjust to their role as mothers of a newborn babies. They were used to a predictable structure and routine. They had been in charge of their work situation, and in control of their environment. Here they were with a tiny baby and for the first time in their lives, they felt they had no control over anything. Their coping skills and self-esteem suffered immeasurably.

One mother, who had been in charge of staff training in a large organisation, reported that no matter how determined she had been each day to shower and get dressed, at lunchtime she was often still in her dressing gown. Her morning cup of tea was cold, and she would cry tears of frustration. It seems the more organised and structured a woman is before the birth, the less she is able to cope with the disorganisation that a new baby brings with it.

I can relate to that. I love having my life in order. Before becoming a mother I was a teacher, so my life was punctuated by bells every forty minutes. This gave structure to my life. Before that I was a student, with a timetable of lectures. My first year at home alone with my baby was a disaster. I felt lonely and isolated. I missed doing things for myself, and the sense of accomplishment it gave me.

I also resented being at home with the baby while my partner was free to work, see friends, and pursue his interests. It was also hard to digest all the conflicting information about how to best take care of the infant.

Should we have a strict routine with our baby?

There are two very different schools of thought about feeding and caring for a newborn. One recommends set feeding times and a rigid schedule of sleeping, bathing and playing. The second suggests 'demand feeding', allowing the baby to choose by expressing his needs. This means that some mothers are feeding twenty-four hours a day. I believe in taking a flexible middle road. Instead of being ready to feed at the baby's first whimper, first see if he has other needs that need satisfying. Some people think if you always go to your baby when he cries you are spoiling him. However, another theory is if you go to your baby whenever he cries, you are showing him that the world is a good, safe and caring place. I tend to agree with this approach, especially early on, when the baby is little.

If you don't go to your baby when he cries, you are teaching him to cry more and feel helpless. However, a habit to avoid is putting the baby on the breast every time he cries. A baby is not hungry every half-hour, and will learn to fall asleep at the breast very quickly. You will then find it difficult to break this habit. Don't do something once that you don't want to repeat. If you make yourself available twenty-four hours a day, you will feel like a slave to your baby. Encourage your partner to participate in parenting. Let him change a nappy and don't snap if it's not perfect. A mother often gets overprotective. Learn to let go of doing everything yourself.

Babies are individuals like us. Some babies may fit in with a mother's need for routine; other mothers may need to adapt to the baby's regime. A battle arises when your baby has irregular needs and you need structure. If you are struggling to establish a routine for your baby, seek help from Karitane or Tresillian (contact details are at the back of the book). Both organisations have trained nurses who will teach you the skills necessary to care for your baby.

Giving birth is a stress that affects your entire psyche as well as your body. Having a baby changes your identity. Your independence is threatened both physically and financially. Some women find it very frightening having a baby who depends on them twenty-four hours a day. Some women also experience considerable physical discomfort during the birth process and take a while to recover from the trauma.

After my first child was born, the doctor stitched up the pudenda nerve when he did my episiotomy. I couldn't sit for six weeks without a rubber tyre and all bodily functions were uncomfortable. I also remember feeling fragile and vulnerable. I felt I needed to be protected. This feeling was in contrast to my former self-sufficiency and strong need for autonomy. The birth itself is an extremely significant life event and I remember swapping birth stories with other women for years after.

I was also determined not to lose my mind once I had a baby. I remember painting every time the baby went to sleep just to connect with my old self. I wanted to make sure my creativity hadn't evaporated with the birth process. Soon after I realised I needed to sleep while the baby did and I abandoned the painting for six months.

Can you overfeed or underfeed a breastfed baby?

Breastfeeding mothers often voice concerns about having enough milk, how frequently to feed and whether they should express milk. Many of us feel anxious about breastfeeding but it is amazing how things settle down once you relax and establish a feeding routine.

The best advice I can give is to let go mentally, emotionally and physically, and enjoy the process. Letting go of anxiety, worry and fear when you are feeding means both you and your baby will find it a satisfying experience. Initially you could choose a comfortable chair in a special room where you feel relaxed. Ask for solitude if you need it. A relaxation tape or soft mellow music may help you unwind. Let friends and relatives know that you need quiet time while you feed. This is your right. Later when you are more confident with the feeding experience, you may feel able to feed with others around.

Ask relatives to do practical things for you, such as the shopping, cooking a meal or tidying the house. You may even ask a relative or friend to watch the baby while you have a bath or go to the hairdresser. Often people want to help, so if you can delegate you are helping them help you.

How does a mother cope with her guilt if she decides not to breastfeed?

We go through periods when breastfeeding is more fashionable. Currently, there is a lot of pressure to breastfeed. However, there are many situations where a mother cannot breastfeed. These may include mastitis (inflammation of the nipple), not enough milk, or inverted, cracked or bleeding nipples. If you do not breastfeed you should not feel guilty or feel that you are depriving your baby.

Of course there are many benefits to breastfeeding, but if you cannot, there are many other ways in which you can be a wonderful mother. Struggling to breastfeed only creates tension in the mother. The baby connects with the tension and both mother and baby become miserable. Giving your baby the bottle when you are relaxed and can enjoy feeding him is far better for the bonding between the mother and baby.

Some mothers don't want to breastfeed. That is also okay. Your baby's well-being, and the relationship between mother and baby, does not depend on breastfeeding or bottle-feeding.

Are there any benefits to bottle-feeding?

Yes, you can let the father or other members of the family help more actively and for longer periods of time. This will give you a bit more freedom. You can catch up with your sleep and claim some time for yourself.

Another thing to be aware of in the first few months is that sleep deprivation is like slow torture! It depresses you. Your mental functioning diminishes and you find it difficult to focus and concentrate.

What can the father do to support the breastfeeding process?

As women and mothers, we need our partners to nurture and protect us. We want them to be rational at a time when we feel vulnerable, emotional and irrational. We want help with the practical domestic tasks and we want to be emotionally self-sufficient. Often this doesn't happen.

Some men now have the task of being the sole provider. They see themselves as working harder than ever, and may not feel like coming home and helping with the domestic tasks. His perception may be that his wife is at home all day, so he cannot understand why she can't manage all the domestic tasks in that time. Lack of understanding between the two creates problems.

Some men become jealous of all the attention a mother gives the new baby. A man may feel he has lost a part of his mate that was totally his before. A bond develops between the mother and the baby, and he may feel left out. Many new fathers take slightly longer to bond with the baby and in the meantime, they feel helpless and isolated. It is vital for a couple to talk about their feelings and realise what is happening. Use humour, rather than anger, to defuse a situation.

Plan how you will handle the baby at night. If the mother is breastfeeding it makes no sense for both of you to have a disturbed night. A father can do little things that make a big difference. He can bring his wife a cup of tea in bed, bring home a take-out dinner, make the evening meal, or clear up the house.

What are some of the problems that a couple has to face when the first baby arrives?

The care of a first child can be quite daunting. We never imagine that this four-kilo bundle will bring about such a time-consuming and exhausting change in our life.

A couple may also feel the weight of responsibility in their new role as parents. Being thrown in at the deep end is frightening, overwhelming and emotionally draining. Often the marriage suffers as a result. Just as the mother was unprepared for tremendous change in her life, the father is also taken by surprise at the changes his partner has gone through. She may have transformed from a calm, capable woman to a sleep-deprived, cranky one, who rejects his affection out of sheer exhaustion.

The couple needs to discuss these changes, and also talk about how they feel. You may want to make some plans for getting help with the chores. Decide what outside services you can afford and how much you can share. If the wife feels her partner understands and is willing to provide help, she will feel nurtured and supported.

JENNY AND MICHAEL WERE HAVING marital problems as their eighteen-month-old son, Adam, a very demanding child, had totally disrupted their lives. He yelled and screamed when he did not get his way. Jenny was exhausted when Michael came home from work. Soon the peaceful life Jenny and Michael had shared prior to Adam's arrival turned into anger, frustration and conflict.

To add to our conflict, Michael thought sex would fix everything, whereas I was always too tired and stressed to enjoy sex,' said Jenny. 'The house was in chaos and we felt there was no fun in our lives.'

We needed to work out some strategies to turn a home filled with fights into a home filled with love and cooperation. During therapy we identified three problems:

- Screaming and yelling at each other, and at Adam.
- Mess and chaos in the home.
- No time for each other.

We drew up a plan to make some positive changes:

- Make peace and calmness in the home a number one priority. Make a decision not to yell and scream at each other or at Adam. Understand that fighting in front of Adam is going to do long-term harm to him.
- Reprogram your lives and put a plan into action.
- Write down a list of chores and decide who will be responsible for each.
- Work on time management. This will allow you to schedule in some 'alone time' when Adam is in bed.
- Save up for babysitting by putting aside all $5 bills that you receive as change from shopping. Then plan a night out. Sit down once a week to re-evaluate the plan and see whether you have stuck to it.

Many women seem to abandon their role as friend and lover once a baby arrives. How do we stop this happening?
Parents need to be aware of potential trouble. Make sure your partner does not feel excluded. Include him in your life. Being a good mother does not necessitate you giving up your role as a wife, friend and lover. Just as you are aware of your child's needs, you need to remain aware of your partner's needs and nurture them.

Each partner has two roles: father and husband, wife and mother. Both partners need to ensure they put equal time and effort into both their roles. A wife has to be careful that she does not put herself in the role of a nanny. She needs to focus also on keeping the intimate part of her relationship alive. The greatest gift parents can give a child is respect for each other and the example of a loving relationship. Have fun together, keep talking to each other, and escape from parenting every now and again.

Another important decision for women to make is when and if they should return to work? What are your thoughts on this?
For many women, returning to work is a financial necessity. Surviving on one income may be too difficult for a prolonged period of time.

Some women decide to go back to work shortly after the birth, but when the time comes they may find they don't want to leave their baby. Many women experience a strong desire to stay close to their baby, especially in the first year. Other women can't wait to get back into their old job, interact with adults again and be mentally stimulated. You have to work out a solution that combines your baby's needs, the needs of your family and what works for you.

You may want to return to work a few months later than you anticipated. Gradual weaning is less stressful for the mother and baby. In the first few months after the birth, a woman may feel vulnerable and less able to cope with the demands of a full-time job and taking care of a baby, even with the help of childcare. The stress of accommodating the demands of a baby, interrupted sleep and change in hormones, need to be taken into account.

What are some of the most challenging changes a woman will face when the baby arrives?

Many women may find themselves on an emotional merry-go-round, happy one moment and tearful the next. These emotions may be hormonal in origin but they can also be a response to stress and lack of sleep.

How you weather the storm depends on many factors. If you are a perfectionist with a great need for order, you will be continually frustrated. Often it is impossible to complete basic tasks and chores without being interrupted by the baby. The basis of stress management is to be able to control the things that are in your power to manage (usually yourself) and to let go of things you cannot control. Avoid struggling in vain and getting nowhere.

What are some steps we can take to cope with stress?

You need to be clear about your priorities. They should be your baby's health, your own well-being, your relationship with your partner, and your family. Give yourself permission to let go of having a meticulous house, pleasing relatives, and other low-priority tasks. Leave all but essential housework, and if you can afford to get someone else to help with the basics, do so.

Think carefully about taking on commitments that use up your energy. Focus on your baby, yourself and your partner. Relax and rest as much as you can. When friends or relatives offer to help, make sure you accept. Don't be a martyr. Give them practical tasks, such as doing the grocery shopping, minding the baby while you do an errand, or cooking a meal. Get as much paid practical help as possible, such as house cleaning, a nappy service, and home-delivered groceries.

Think about joining a mothers' group so you can connect and share experiences with women in similar situations. Accept that the first few months are the toughest. Each day the baby will become easier to manage, as your skills and confidence increase.

When your baby sleeps, rest yourself, or do things that give you a sense of personal satisfaction. This may be reading a book, taking a long, hot bath or chatting to a friend. Simplify your life as much as possible. Focus on the positives. Enjoy the time, as these early stages pass quickly. As you gain confidence, it all becomes easier.

How can we learn to go with the flow?

You can't force someone to eat or sleep. Babies are no exception. Try to respect the baby's needs, and respond to them as soon as possible. This will give the baby the message that the world is a safe place.

What about the post-natal blues?

On the third or fourth day after giving birth, a woman may feel teary and emotional. This is hormonal and doesn't last long. However, there are women who go on to experience post-natal depression. This is a longer-lasting condition, characterised by specific features. It may go on for weeks or months and you must get professional help to deal with the situation. We have discussed aspects of this syndrome in the chapter on depression. Some of the symptoms you may experience include the following:

- You don't look forward to doing enjoyable things.
- You tend to blame yourself unnecessarily.
- You feel anxious and worried for no good reason.
- You may feel scared and panicky.
- You may feel sad, miserable or tearful.
- You may be at risk of harming yourself.
- You may feel disconnected from your baby and that makes you feel like a bad mother.
- You may have problems eating or sleeping.
- You could be at risk of harming your child.

What do you do if you discover you are experiencing several of these symptoms?
It is vital you go to your GP and get a referral to a psychiatrist. You may need medication and counselling to get you through this time. You also need some practical support, such as help with your housework and taking care of the baby. There are a number of psychologists and psychiatrists who specialise in the area of post-natal depression.

What are your views on the baby being in bed with the parents?
I know this area is a minefield of varying opinions, but I feel strongly that a baby should not be in the same bed as the parents, or in the same room. I have come across too many mothers who listen to the baby's breathing all night and they cannot relax. I believe that people need personal space and boundaries. I like the idea of the marital bed being the domain of the couple and the baby having a crib or cot in a nearby room. This enables a couple to resume their relationship more easily and to have some personal time.

Toolbox

- Don't panic if you do not experience maternal love straight away. It may take a little time to develop.
- If you struggle with breastfeeding or don't enjoy it, don't feel guilty. Your baby will be fine with bottle-feeding.
- Don't feed your baby every time he cries. He may need reassurance, a cuddle, a nappy change, or she may be crying from sheer tiredness.
- Let your baby learn to put himself to sleep. If you always rock him and pick him up, he will not learn to fall asleep on his own.
- If you experience any symptoms of post-natal depression, get help.
- Try to conserve your energy. Your priorities should be your baby, yourself and your partner.
- Accept help if relatives or friends offer it. Ask them to do practical things.
- Have as much rest as possible, especially in the first three months. Broken sleep can make you feel irritable, anxious, and even depressed.
- Decide when and if you want to return to work..
- Don't abandon your role as wife, friend and lover when the baby arrives. Nurture your relationship with your partner as well.

chapter fourteen

Toddlers and Pre-schoolers: Discipline and Boundaries

THE RAISING OF TODDLERS AND pre-school children is usually either a nightmare, fraught with screaming matches, or a time of wonder and enjoyment. Little children have the potential to learn an enormous amount and give their parents a great deal of pleasure. Taking care of them, however, requires focus, consistency and a great deal of patience and energy.

You can empower yourself with skills and understanding to make this time a positive period, filled with growth and adventure. You can also view it as one of the most trying experiences of your life – the choice is yours.

What do we need to know to cope with this next phase of parenting?

You need to be aware that your toddler is a self-centred individual. He will only see things from his point of view. He often demands constant attention and becomes angry when his needs are not met immediately. He may experience difficulty in sharing and have not yet learnt to be patient. He may have a limited awareness of danger and see himself as invincible.

As the parent of a toddler, you have a full-time occupation. Toddlers find it difficult to regulate their own behaviour. They will keep going until they run out of steam and then get extremely tired and cranky. Bear in mind that toddlers do not behave selfishly on purpose. They are simply unaware of other people's feelings.

As a toddler begins to explore his environment, he may get into dangerous situations because he does not understand the consequences of his actions. Parents have to be vigilant in such a way that they protect toddlers from danger, but still encourage them to explore and become independent. It can be a fine line.

What are some of the traps that parents fall into and how can they avoid them?

In today's world, parental stress is a major problem. There is less time to devote to children. Parents are often trying to juggle family and work. This stress results in them taking the easier option and giving in to their toddlers. A part-time mum often does this because she feels guilty. In her stressed state, she feels it is easier to give in than put up with her toddler's tantrums. Inadvertently, she teaches her child, 'If you throw a tantrum or whine enough, you can have what you want.'

She then finds herself with bigger problems. She may issue repeated threats and warnings, which she then doesn't carry out. She may yell. She may even resort to smacking her child for non-compliance. She may be inconsistent in how she manages her toddler. Saying 'yes' to a situation one day, and 'no' to the same situation the next confuses a child.

How can we begin to deal with some of these areas?

I believe toddlers need consistency. They need boundaries, limits and clear guidelines for each situation. They will benefit from having simple, clear instructions, and rewards for positive behaviour. It is essential that parents agree on a consistent line of action so that their child doesn't receive conflicting messages. In other words, the couple should reach agreement on what behaviour they expect, and stick to it.

BELINDA AND PETER WERE CONCERNED about three-year old Kelly's behaviour, which they described as 'out of control'. Tantrums had become part of her daily routine. By giving into her, Belinda had inadvertently rewarded Kelly's tantrums and taught her that throwing a tantrum meant she would get her own way. This worked particularly well for Kelly in a public place such as a supermarket, where Belinda was so embarrassed that she gave in much quicker than at home.

I realised that yelling at Kelly to stop her tantrums did not work. The yelling was just part of the noise, and Kelly didn't even hear me.' Belinda also learned that when a child is out of control, it means the parent is out of control. She had to learn new ways of communicating with her daughter in order to change her behaviour.

Belinda needed to be patient. She had been giving into Kelly for several months, so it was going to take Kelly some time to realise that there was no more pay-off for her tantrums. If Belinda gave in even once, the behaviour would worsen. I told Belinda: 'If you feel you cannot always resist giving in, don't begin this process. Wait until you have the determination to resist giving in.

It was important that Belinda and Peter supported each other, showing Kelly that they meant business and being consistent. The trick was to be more persistent than Kelly, not to yell at her, and to take every opportunity to praise desirable behaviour.

I know the most challenging problems at this age are temper tantrums. How can we deal with them effectively?

Tantrums vary from a frustrated child who cries and yells for a few minutes, to a child kicking, screaming and crying for forty-five minutes. Most tantrums thrown by children under three are uncontrolled, and may be a result of the frustration the child is experiencing as he learns to cope with his environment. The tantrum is often an indirect way of expressing frustrated needs.

If a child is overtired, hungry, overstimulated or excited, he may not be able to control his emotions. He may not be getting enough sleep, and become grouchy or tense. He may be receiving too much attention, or be coping with too many restrictions. A child requires space and time to exercise his independence. He also needs consistency, love and positive attention.

There are various ways in which to respond to a tantrum. The child may need to be distracted. The child may need sympathy or cuddling in order to redirect his attention. He may need to be left alone until the worst of his feelings have passed.

It is vital that you never give in to a child's tantrum. If early tantrums provide the child with a reward, he will use tantrums to get what he wants in the future. It becomes a powerful tool for manipulation. If you comfort and sympathise without giving in, you will not reinforce the tantrums. Tantrums can be thrown on purpose to obtain positive or negative attention. Usually there are no tears with these tantrums and they can be stopped at the will of the child.

If a child is throwing a manipulative tantrum, completely ignore him and his behaviour. Do not talk to him, look at him, or comfort him in any way. Try not to look tense or upset by the performance. If it is impossible to remain calm, leave the room. Do not punish your child during the tantrum. Once he has stopped the tantrum, reinforce the positive behaviour. Do not discuss the previous behaviour and do not give him what he wanted.

This approach will take time to be effective. The behaviour may get worse initially as he tests you out. Some children hold their breath during a temper tantrum. Try not to let the child see your fright. Attempt to relax or distract him before he gets upset. Tantrums are not unusual but you need to deal with them firmly. It is crucial that you pretend not to be upset and that you deal with your toddler firmly but with understanding.

What do we do if the child has a tantrum in a public place?

A child is more likely to have a tantrum if she is hungry or tired. Don't take a tired child to the supermarket. You are asking for trouble. Take snacks on a long outing. If he does have a tantrum, try to move him to a less public place. If this is not possible, ignore the people around and let the tantrum take its course, rather than give in to him.

What else can we do to create an environment that minimises behaviour problems?

Children thrive on consistency and routines. A predictable environment enables a toddler to develop self-control and trust his environment. The child will keep testing. If you continue to be consistent, he will then feel safe and secure.

Activities need to be appropriate for your child's level of development. If we rush our child around, don't give him enough quiet time or overstimulate him, we can expect him to become overwhelmed and act up. Children also need time to disconnect from an activity before they move onto the next. Give him a warning that he is reaching the end of one activity. He will then feel more in control, as he knows what is happening next. Routines help children develop a clear picture of the future and give them inner security. Limits also make them feel safe.

I believe in having a few rules rather than many. Rules should be specific and clear. They should be reasonable for a child of toddler age, and they should be enforceable.

As adults we can introduce changes to the environment if we think things may get out of hand. Ignore negative behaviour and reward positive behaviour. Tell your child exactly what behaviour is required.

How do you get a two-year-old to go to bed at night without a drama?

Set a time for your child to go to bed. For example, 'When the clock says eight, it's time for you to go to bed.' Establish some going-to-bed rituals. This may include some quiet time with you or your partner, time for stories and time for some hugging and affection. If your child continues to cry or argue when it's time for bed, tell him that it's bedtime in a firm, loving tone.

If you know your child is reluctant to go to bed, you could try the following exercise. Before he starts to cry, explain to your child, 'If you are quiet when I put you to bed, you can listen to your favourite nursery rhyme tape. But if you cry, you won't be able to hear the tape'.

Establish a consistent bedtime and wake-up time. The hour before bedtime should be a calm and relaxing time without rough or excitable play. The actual bedtime routine should involve about twenty minutes with one parent who provides warmth and comfort. As your child gets older, you may consider adjusting his daytime schedule so that he is tired at bedtime. This may mean eliminating the afternoon nap or moving it to an earlier time.

Give your child a five-minute warning before bedtime. Make it a special time. Don't take phone calls. Just give your child 100 per cent undivided attention. Let him know bedtime is approaching. He will then look forward to this special time rather than resist it.

DON'T MAKE THREATS YOU CAN'T CARRY OUT

THINK BEFORE YOU THREATEN. REMEMBER THAT SOME THREATS COULD PUNISH YOU MORE THAN YOUR CHILD. MAKE A LIST OF CONSEQUENCES THAT WORK FOR YOUR CHILD, AND ARE APPROPRIATE FOR THE BEHAVIOUR. THIS WILL MINIMISE THE RISK OF MAKING UNREALISTIC OR UNENFORCEABLE THREATS.

What happens if he gets out of bed?

It is important to understand the source of bedtime problems. Firstly, your child may experience fears around separation. He may be tense and find it difficult to relax. This may also be an opportunity for your child to control or manipulate you. If bedtime becomes a struggle, you need to create and implement a strategy. It may take one to two weeks of determined effort to change bad bedtime habits but it is worth the energy if it relieves you from nightly struggles.

Once a child turns two, a change to the bedtime routine requires firmness on your part. After your bedtime ritual of stories and hugs, kiss your child goodnight and walk out of the room. One school of thought says if your child cries, allow him to cry for ten minutes. Then return to his room and explain firmly that he has to go to sleep. Leave the room again and allow the child to cry for fifteen minutes. By this time he will be asleep. If not, return every fifteen minutes. Not every parent can implement this method, but for those who can, it works well.

When my son was two and a half, I tried this technique. I have to confess it was very difficult for the first three nights. He cried hysterically. He made himself sick and he banged his head against the cot. But in the end I won the battle and bedtime stopped being such a battleground. I felt liberated.

What do you do you do if your child wakes up during the night?
If your child wakes up crying in the night, he may be having a nightmare. When he calls you, wait a while before you go to him. He may go back to sleep. When you go to check on him, use a minimal amount of communication. Reassure him that everything is fine. If he has a cuddly toy, give it to him for comfort. Be firm, and reassure your child you are close by.

If he wants to share his dream, listen and reassure him. Explain to him that his dream was not real and encourage him to go back to sleep. Tell him briefly about some fun activity that he will do the next day. This distracts him and gives him something to look forward to. Don't give him snacks or treats. At all costs, avoid letting him come into your bed in the middle of the night. This is a very hard habit to break.

Setting up a reward system, such as a lucky dip, can work very well to change a child's bad sleeping habits. A lucky dip consists of little toys or treats wrapped in different coloured paper and placed in a transparent plastic bag. Keep this out of the child's reach but within his view. When you put him to bed, say to him, 'If you don't wake Mummy or Daddy, you can have a present from the lucky dip in the morning'. Be confident and consistent in how you handle bedtime and nightmares. It is important that a child learns to how to self-soothe and fall asleep by himself.

When a child is ill, if you are travelling or visitors are coming to stay, his routine may be disrupted. Make sure you resume the original routine as soon as possible. Bad habits develop quickly.

How do we cope with our older child when we bring a new baby home?

Parents may feel guilty because they are not spending as much time with their older child as they used to. This guilt may encourage them to remove some of the limits they have put in place. The result of this is that the older child actually becomes insecure and starts testing his boundaries. Parents can expect some anger and aggression from their older child. They should keep most of the limits in place, however, as this maintains a sense of security.

When I brought my new baby home, I introduced special reading times when I breastfed the baby.

That's excellent. Another good idea is a basket of special toys that you bring out for the older child to play with while you are breastfeeding. Change around the toys so that there is a surprise element in the basket. Avoid polarising the relationship so that the older child always goes off with Dad and you stay with the baby. You should also have special one-on-one time with your older child. Leave Dad at home with the baby and take your toddler to the park.

How can we make it easier for the toddler to cope with the baby?

Start preparing your toddler for the new arrival. Talk to him about the baby growing in your tummy. Explain that you will be away in hospital for a few days. You could prepare a tape with messages for him while you are away. Leave a photo of yourself next to his bed and something special of yours that he could look after. This will make him feel important and trusted. It will also allow him to feel connected to you.

Since the new baby will receive attention and gifts, have a few treats ready for your older child. Make sure that grandparents still make a fuss of your first child. Encourage your older child to help you with the baby at bathtime. Also ask him to do small errands for you so that he feels important. Teach your toddler to be gentle with the baby.

It's natural for children to compete for attention, so expect some jealousy and rivalry when the new baby arrives. Most toddlers enjoy looking at their own baby photographs. Tell him, 'You are a big boy now. You can help me look after the baby'.

What's the best way to discipline a toddler, tantrums aside?

I feel very strongly that you should not smack a child. There are a number of reasons why you should resist smacking.

- Imagine someone three times your size raising his hand and hitting you. How would you feel? Would it result in a positive relationship with that giant?
- As a parent you are a model of good or bad behaviour. Your child learns by watching you. If you hit your child when you are upset, you teach your child to resort to hitting when things don't go her way.
- Physical violence is a quick fix to anger and frustration. There are always days when everything goes wrong. Every parent has a breaking point. We could easily lose our cool

and hit a lot harder than we mean to. Make a commitment not to smack.

- When I worked in the area of child abuse, I came across parents who severely harmed their children. It was hard to understand parents hurting their own children in this way. These parents were not able to control their anger when faced with their distressed children. Some of these children even needed to be brought into casualty for treatment.

How can you get your toddler to do as he is told without smacking him?

Raising a child without discipline is like driving a car without steering it. The result could be disastrous. To be effective, discipline must be imposed with love and affection. Discipline is not punishment. Children misbehave most when they are tired, hungry and bored. Here are a few principles to remember:

- Distraction is the best tactic for an eighteen-month-old toddler.
- Issue one instruction at a time. Be specific.
- If a child has broken a rule or exceeded limits, tell him immediately.
- Always explain carefully to a child what he has done wrong.
- Don't threaten unless you can carry out the threat.
- By disciplining a child you socialise him and teach him self-control.
- Instead of having too many rules, have a few. Keep them brief and stick to them.
- It helps if a child has a regular routine so that he can make sense of his world. This gives him security.
- Praise and rewards work better than punishment. So wherever possible give positive feedback for behaviour.
- Never call your child stupid, bad, clumsy or ugly. Criticise the behaviour and not the child.

What are some ways we can deal with negative behaviour?

Time-out is a useful technique, although you need to use it as a tool for specific situations. It is vital to warn a child only once, that if his behaviour continues he will be having time-out as a consequence. You can send a child to his room for time-out. It is less of a punishment and more of an opportunity to separate yourself from your child. It allows both you and your child to calm down.

When you deal with negative behaviour, ensure that the discipline you apply has immediate significance. For example, if your child was told not to come inside with muddy shoes but ignores your instruction, make him wipe up the mess. When you punish your child, do not withdraw love as a form of punishment but let him know that you are upset with his behaviour.

Try to limit the range of punishable behaviours. Let the small things go and focus on a few negative behaviours. Make sure you and your partner agree with the discipline applied. Do not disagree in front of your child. You can debate later when your child is out of earshot.

How can we teach our children to understand their feelings?

Use the words 'sad', 'happy' and 'angry' to describe how people feel, so that your child learns to identify feelings and make distinctions between them. Help him verbalise his feelings instead of acting out his anger. Encourage your child to practise labelling his own feelings so that he can express his emotions as they occur.

I read stories to my children that highlighted different feelings. One book was called Joan is Angry. *We would make the connection between the character in the story and my children's own feelings. If my daughter lost her temper, I would ask, 'Are you feeling angry like Joan?'*

How can we encourage our children to develop problem-solving skills?

If your child comes to you with a problem, no matter how small by adult standards, don't ever trivialise it. At the age of three or four, your child may not have the verbal skills necessary to resolve an argument. Instead, he may use physical force or tears to express his feelings. As a parent, you can help your child practise his existing verbal skills.

The best thing that you can do for your child is teach him how to solve his own problems in a non-aggressive way. This will give him the confidence to communicate in an assertive way. An important part of conflict resolution is to explain that no violence is acceptable, no matter how angry, frustrated or upset the child is feeling. Spend time talking to your child about feelings. Show him how his behaviour affects others. Empathy is difficult for a child to understand.

How can we use rewards effectively?

To encourage positive behaviour, parents should reward their children. These rewards should not be things that money can buy. Rather, they should be extra attention from parents – smiles, kisses, hugs, praise or specific feedback relating to the positive behaviour. These positive responses reinforce a child's actions and help him make sense of his world.

Rewards do not always succeed in making your child act in a desired way, but they do reinforce the behaviour once executed. There is a difference between bribes and rewards. We usually offer bribes when we want quick results and we do not have the energy to explain why. Here is an example of a bribe:

Mum: 'It's time to go home.'
Child: 'I don't want to go home. I'm having a good time.'
Mum: 'If you come, I'll buy you an ice-cream.'

If your child then says, 'I don't want an ice-cream', you are stuck. A better approach to a bribe is to say, 'We are leaving in five minutes, please get ready to go home'.

'I don't want to go home, I'm having a good time.'
'I can see you are having fun playing with Zoe. Would you like to invite her to play with you tomorrow?'
'Yes,'
'So say goodbye and you'll see her tomorrow.'

If we offer bribes frequently, the child may always expect something tangible in return for every action. We all use bribes when we run out of time, energy or patience. Try to focus on rewards. Give as much positive feedback to your child as possible and he will blossom in that environment. A bribe is conditional, whereas a reward is given after the positive behaviour.

How can we teach our children to organise themselves?

Mothers often come to me complaining that their children dawdle and forget things. They become distracted and daydream. This makes simple outings such as getting ready for pre-school a nightmare. A child often forgets his belongings because he daydreams and is not focused.

You can teach your child simple organisational skills. Create an environment where everything has its place. Put books in one place, puzzles in another and organise their clothes. Show these processes to your child. Encourage him to help in returning items to their appropriate places. Communicate how things are kept and where.

Explain the progression of the day's events to your child. Run through the daily schedule so that he knows what to expect. Transitions can be difficult for a young child, so guide him through changes of activities gradually. When it is almost dinnertime, for example, let him know that playing time is coming to an end. Be consistent. Routine helps young children make sense of their world. Teach your child how to be ready on time by going through the activities that need to be completed. For example, 'We are going to get dressed, have breakfast, brush our teeth and then go to school'. Create a routine and stick to it. This discipline will help your child later in life.

DON'T HIT YOUR CHILD

SMACKING DOES YOUR CHILD MORE HARM THAN GOOD. YOU MAY RELEASE SOME OF YOUR ANGER AND FRUSTRATION, BUT YOU ARE TEACHING YOUR CHILD THAT WHEN YOU ARE ANGRY OR DON'T GET YOUR WAY, YOU CAN HIT SOMEONE. A CHILD WHO IS SMACKED OFTEN MAY BECOME AGGRESSIVE WITH OTHER CHILDREN.

How do we teach a child good manners?

A child learns manners and respect by observing how his parents treat others. If they are courteous and polite to people, always saying 'please' and 'thank you', the child will emulate this behaviour. Manners are a means of showing a child how to control his impulses and develop an inner voice. For example, little children tend to interrupt conversations when they need to say something. It is important to teach them to wait until whoever is speaking has finished talking before they speak.

If a child is rude or disobeys, be prepared to use consequences. With children three and older, you can use one warning and then apply time-out for a negative behaviour. As with all discipline, focus on the positive. Keep rewarding good manners and positive behaviour. Keep instructions simple. Stick to a few rules and be consistent with these. Children thrive in an environment that provides them with love and affection as well as security and limits. Use punishment as a last resort.

Toolbox

- Understand the difference between punishment and discipline.
- Toddlers need consistency. Have a few rules and stick to them.
- Give toddlers clear guidelines, limits and boundaries.
- Never give in to temper tantrums, otherwise they will be used as a powerful tool to manipulate you.
- Create a bedtime ritual and make that time a special opportunity for you to connect with your child.
- If your child wakes in the night, do not allow him into your bed. Go to him, soothe him and let him fall asleep in his own bed.
- Read books to your child as often as possible.
- Never smack your toddler. It may seem like the easy way out, but in the long term it is not effective.
- Distraction is the best policy with toddlers.
- Praise and reward works better than punishment.

chapter fifteen

Primary and School-Aged Children

JACQUI AND ROBERT, AND THEIR eight-year-old twins, Samantha and Vanessa, came to see me because the family was in chaos. Jacqui worked from 9.30 am until 2.30 pm, and found it difficult to get the girls' cooperation to get ready on time in the morning.

The family needed rules that were appropriate to a specific age, and enforceable. These rules included cooperation, morning and evening routines, chores and homework. The girls helped with suggestions regarding the morning routine. The list included making the bed, getting dressed, brushing teeth and hair, having breakfast. They were so enthusiastic that they wanted to make a list for the afternoon and the evening as well.

Jacqui and Robert could hardly believe the level of cooperation at home. 'Our task was to praise the girls' behaviour and reward them with special things to do with them. On the first weekend, the girls asked Jacqui to supervise them while they baked muffins.' As the girls were included in the planning of tasks, they were very willing to cooperate in carrying out the tasks, and the home became a peaceful environment.

From the age of five or six, when a child starts school, her parents may play a less significant role in her daily life. The forces that come into play are the school, friends and outside influences.

One of the challenges of bringing up children today is to be able to steer them in the right direction, despite competing influences. Our task as parents at this stage is to foster and encourage social independence in our child. At the same time, we need to ensure that we are instilling family values and guiding our children, while building their self-esteem and confidence.

This period also allows parents to gauge their success at teaching their children to adhere to family rules. If at this stage it is the child who is the boss and not the parents, you may be in for some challenging moments. It is vital that parents continue to set limits, manage the child's behaviour and implement discipline.

As a child becomes independent, she will test her parents' authority. Finding a balance between encouraging independence and reigning in unacceptable behaviour takes energy and commitment.

What do we need to know to equip ourselves for this stage?

Parents need to give a child unconditional love, even when they are disciplining her. Never reject a child, or withdraw love as a punishment for misbehaviour. Also avoid showing love as a reward for achievement only.

If your child feels that you only praise her when she achieves, she could feel insecure. She may feel that if she does not live up to your expectations, you will not love her. Your child not only needs to know that you love her, but that you like her. Maintain a close bond of affection and encourage her to talk to you.

What's the best way of keeping the lines of communication open?

There is nothing more valuable that you can give your child than time and undivided attention. In today's world, many families have two working parents, so time is a very precious commodity. I feel, however, that sometimes even full-time mothers fail to give their children undivided attention. It is important to make time to enjoy a shared activity without distractions, or go out for a meal or a walk together. Half an hour of one-on-one time, at least three times a week, will benefit you and your child enormously.

Discuss with your child what activities she would like to share. Make that time special. Don't take phone calls or allow interruptions. Listen when your child talks to you. Let her know that you have heard her.

Often when your child comes home from school, you are busy Stop your activities for ten minutes and listen to the stories of her day. Try to learn to read clues from her behaviour. What kind of day has she had? Does she look stressed or tired? If she looks upset, gently question her and encourage her to express her feelings. You may want to say, 'You look upset, would you like to tell me what is upsetting you?'

Should families have rules?

Every family needs some rules, and the earlier you teach your child a clear set of rules the sooner she will learn what is expected of her. When she starts school and starts to visit friends she will soon discover that different families have different rules.

What are the characteristics of a rule?

Each rule or limit should have a simple directive. It should have reason and purpose. Children can accept rules if there is a logical purpose behind them. There should be consequences if the behaviour is inappropriate and an agreement about whether there is a warning or not. Explain the consequences to the child. Set the limits in advance, don't overload the limits, and remember that each behaviour rule should be age-appropriate.

Another important aspect of family rules is to make them impersonal. For example, 'No-one in this house hits or smacks, because it hurts'; 'No-one in this house jumps on the couch or other furniture'. Make sure you and your spouse discuss these rules before you share them with the children.

At what age can children start to help around the house?

I believe children can start helping from a very young age. Make sure you give them tasks that are appropriate to their age and level of motor coordination. A four- or five-year-old can learn to set the table and tidy up her toys. As she gets older, you can gradually increase the range of chores.

Much depends upon the attitude towards chores in the house. Are chores seen as a shared responsibility or only Mum's domain? Your attitude towards chores can influence the way your children perceive gender identity. You could also consider whether your children should have specific assigned responsibilities, or if they are only required to help now and again.

In my experience, it is much better to assign specific responsibilities to each child on a roster system, and to encourage the concept of shared responsibility – so they don't see Mum as the slave.

I agree with you. Children need to learn the value of work. Having regular chores that are their responsibility means they can learn skills, and become competent and independent. This often starts in pre-school years, with children encouraged to take care of their belongings and tidy their toys. By the time a child is eight or nine she can actively participate in household chores. This has obvious benefits for you and your partner as well.

LOOK OUT FOR POSITIVES AND PRAISE YOUR CHILDREN

BUILD YOUR CHILD'S SELF-ESTEEM BY GIVING POSITIVE FEEDBACK AND PRAISE. FOR EXAMPLE, SAY, 'YOU HAVE PAINTED A BEAUTIFUL PICTURE. I LOVE THE BRIGHT COLOURS YOU CHOSE', OR 'THANK YOU FOR TIDYING UP YOUR ROOM. IT WAS VERY HELPFUL'. PRAISE WORKS BETTER THAN PUNISHMENT, WHICH SHOULD BE A LAST RESORT.

You can introduce a range of chores to your children at the same time, allocating age-appropriate tasks to each child. As you say, it is a good idea to draw up a family roster. Explain to your children that by sharing the responsibilities, you will all have more time as a family to do fun activities. They may protest that none of their friends has to help at home. Explain that each family has different rules and that these are the rules in your family.

How do you go about creating a roster?

Get the whole family to sit down together. Take a big sheet of paper and brainstorm all the tasks that need to be done each week. Items on the list may include shopping, cooking, laundry, putting away washing, feeding the dog, and unloading the dishwasher. Assign jobs to each family member, including Mum and Dad. Some jobs could be allocated on a weekly basis.

Let the children know that once they have been given a chore, it is their responsibility to execute it. Reward and praise their efforts. You may also link the roster into a pocket money or other reward system.

I don't think it's a good idea for children to learn to only do things for money.

There are times when giving financial reward, for pocket money, works. This is true for older children who have no history of sharing the responsibility for chores. A recent client of mine was a single mother, whose three teenage sons did no household chores. So we drew up a list of chores, and assigned a monetary value to each chore. The boys were then able to earn their pocket money. In this situation the system worked well, but it's not necessary to give money for chores to young children.

It is vital to have consequences in place if chores are not done, such as prohibiting television, withholding pocket money or playtime. To make the system work effectively, set times by which the chores need to be done. Don't hassle or nag your child. You may give one reminder each day and then withdraw so that the child can be responsible for his own task. You need to be specific about what that task is. For example, putting all clothes and toys away in the cupboards, not just 'tidy your room'. As children mature, they will be ready to undertake more complex tasks.

How much time should children allocate to chores?
Chores should not be too time-consuming. Children still need time for play, hobbies, homework and sport. As they get older they can be given more chores. The idea behind chores is to help your child become responsible, to feel capable and to not take things for granted. It helps to be part of a team that cooperates and works together.

You obviously believe in pocket money, but at what age should it start?
Yes, I'm a great believer in pocket money. I believe giving children a small regular allowance teaches them to manage money. It gives children an opportunity to save, to learn the value of money and how to spend money wisely. It is vital that a pocket money system is consistent and age-appropriate. From the age of seven or eight, a child can receive a regular weekly small amount of cash, which she can save or spend.

Discuss with your child what she is expected to use her money for. It may cover tuck shop purchases, sweets and small toys. Each family will decide on the amount, according to what they can afford. As a child gets older you should increase the amount of pocket money.

Should you encourage children to save?
Some children find it difficult to save and others want to save most of their pocket money. Either way, giving pocket money to your children is a great opportunity to teach them the pleasure of spending, and the rewards of saving for a special item. For

example, my ten-year-old grandson recently saved some pocket money so that he could have some holiday spending money. You could also encourage your child to put a few coins into a moneybox each week, which she could then donate to her favourite charity. At some schools children are encouraged to bring a few coins for charity each week. An effective pocket money system gives children an opportunity to become independent and skilled at making financial decisions.

I think one of the big issues for parents of primary school children is how much television to allow them to watch.

This is indeed a very big question! Television can be a source of continual conflict unless clear guidelines are set. It has a major impact on children and can absorb an enormous slice of their time. Television can be used in a positive way, to educate children, but this requires vigilance. First of all, decide how many hours per week you will allow your child to watch television. It may be an hour a day during the week and longer on the weekends, for example.

Allow your child to select the programs she wants to watch. Make sure they are suitable, and explain the ground rules for watching television. These may include no TV until homework is finished, no TV at dinner times, and only the programs discussed can be watched. Don't leave the TV on as background. The same rule applies to computers. The more time spent watching television or playing computer games, the less time there is for socialising, playing and reading.

Exposure to television is often linked to the issue of family values. Children get exposed to many conflicting ideas today. How can we be sure they learn basic values?

I think it is vital to talk to your children about family values. You can start early with young children and then deepen the discussion as they get older. First, parents need to discuss which values they want to share with their children. These may include honesty, compassion, courage, self-discipline, loyalty, respect, consideration for others, kindness and fair play. Teaching children these values helps them develop into moral, caring adults.

Parents also need to know that the most important thing is how their children act. Children learn by example. Telling your child to respect the truth is of no value when she hears you tell lies, even small ones. As parents, you have to live your life the way you want your child to behave.

DON'T BE OVERPROTECTIVE

WHEN YOU DO THINGS FOR YOUR CHILD THAT HE COULD DO FOR HIMSELF, YOU ARE GIVING HIM THE MESSAGE THAT HE CAN'T LOOK AFTER HIMSELF. ALLOW HIM TO DO THINGS INDEPENDENTLY. TEACH HIM TO MAKE DECISIONS. GIVE HIM THE CONFIDENCE TO TRY NEW ACTIVITIES AND NOT TO BE FEARFUL OF DIFFERENT SITUATIONS. BUT MAKE SURE EXPECTATIONS ARE REALISTIC, OTHERWISE YOU WILL BE SETTING HIM UP TO FAIL.

There is a useful book by Dominic Cappello, called *Ten Talks Parents Must Have with Their Children About Sex and Character*. Cappello maintains that we should not only have these conversations with our children, but we should write our family values down and post them on the refrigerator as a reminder.

How do we go about having one of these talks?

One option, once parents have defined the guiding principles they want their children to follow, is to set aside time for the talk. Allocate about twenty minutes in a quiet place. Turn the television off and take the phone off the hook.

Define your family values for your children and let them write them down. Give examples. During the course of daily life, point out to your children any examples of these values put into practice. You may see them illustrated in a movie, a story or in a real life event. Go over the incident, highlighting the value in question. Explain to your children how value builds character.

Another option that I adopted in my family was a more informal approach. I had long discussions with them at bedtime, during which they told me about their day. I used their experiences to talk to them about relevant values.

What if your child asks you awkward questions?

Parents are entitled to have a private life. Set your own personal boundaries and share as much as you are comfortable with. You can be truthful without telling everything. Age-appropriate answers are necessary, especially when it comes to sex.

At primary school age, it may be useful to establish family rules about appropriate sexual behaviour. Discuss with your child the concept of personal space and boundaries. Explain to her that no-one may invade her personal space without permission. She is entitled to privacy and certain activities are only performed in private.

Most families have differing views on nudity and what is acceptable. Discuss with your child the possibility of peer pressure in certain situations. Encourage her to think for herself and not to follow the crowd in order to be accepted. Explain to her that every family has a different set of values and she should be clear on what her family values are.

Can you list some of the values that we can focus on at primary school age?

When I was a single mother, I was determined to give my children clear guidelines. I focused on the importance of honesty. I told my children it was essential they always tell me the truth. I encouraged them to be thoughtful to others, and to have compassion for those less privileged than them. I insisted on them showing respect for those who were older, such as parents and grandparents. I also encouraged them to achieve, always doing their personal best.

We should take every opportunity to teach our children values. If your child comes home from school feeling upset because her friend cheated while playing a game, for example, say to her, 'It is so upsetting when somebody cheats. You seem hurt by your friend's behaviour'. Then discuss with her how important fair play is. Remind her that she should never cheat, as cheating is unfair to others.

How do we handle sibling rivalry? I know my brother and I fought like crazy as kids and so did my two children. For parents, this can be very stressful. How do we prevent it, and how do we cope?

Make an effort to love each child for their unique qualities. Express affection for all your children. Love them for their differences. If one child is more of an academic achiever, find ways to give the other child recognition and self-esteem. Treat all your children fairly and avoid comparing one child with another, because it breeds resentment. Each child has her own special qualities. Become aware of any subtle favouritism.

Spend some time with each child every day. Allow your child to be the focus of your attention and really listen to her. This is an opportunity for connecting. The more you give of yourself, the less your children will compete with each other.

Give each child as much privacy and space as possible. If you have the extra space, give each child their own room. There can be problems if they share – one child may be messy and the other tidy, one may want to spend quiet time and the other want noise. Don't dress your children identically, especially if they are twins. Allow them to choose their own clothes, colour and style to express their individuality. Encourage your children to have separate experiences. It is healthy for them to have different friends, hobbies, likes and dislikes.

Living in a family harmoniously means having respect for each other and good communication. Nurture generosity between the siblings.

What do we do when our children squabble?

Try to ignore the small disputes and let them work out a resolution for themselves, especially if they are evenly matched. When you do intervene, try to be an impartial negotiator. Try to teach them effective problem-solving skills.

What if they express really strong feelings, like 'I hate you'?

Let them know that it is normal to feel as if they hate their brother or sister at that moment. However, acknowledge that it is a hurtful thing to say. Allow your children to express their feelings without feeling guilty, but don't allow punching or physical violence. Here is a case where two brothers were very jealous of each other.

BRENDA AND TONY HAVE TWO sons, Justin, nine, and Sam, eleven, who are very jealous of each other. Though their emotions are normal, the arguments were exhausting their parents. 'They were continually fighting and driving us mad. The jealousy was making the boys miserable, angry, possessive and difficult to live with.'

We came up with various strategies. Three nights per week for half an hour was to be 'special time'. During this time Brenda and Tony took turns spending time with Justin and Sam. One day Brenda played a card game with Justin, while Tony, in another room, played a board game with Sam. The next time it was Sam's turn with Brenda, and Justin's turn with Tony. The phone was not answered during this time and there were no negative discussions about their behaviour. This was to be a very positive time.

When arguments between the boys arose, Tony and Brenda told them it was okay to feel angry with each other, but not okay to punch each other. Brenda and Tony soon discovered the individual strengths and skills in each boy that they could focus on.

Their behaviour at home quickly improved. The arguments between the boys did not stop, but they certainly diminished. Tony was surprised when the boys asked him whether they could have an extra half-hour with him for a joint activity, so they could play a game together.

Is it of any value to separate children if they fight constantly?

For a while, I think it's a good idea to make practical arrangements to keep children apart. This can be done in a constructive way. Organise different after-school activities and encourage them to have separate friends. Although this may prove more time-consuming, the benefits will be worth the effort, namely peaceful and happy children. With less time spent together, along with separate activities so they are not competing with each other, the animosity will probably settle down and they will be much happier in each other's company.

What is at the core of sibling rivalry?

Most sibling rivalry is underscored by the strong emotion of jealousy; when one child really wants something or someone that another child has. Jealousy may stem from insecurity and a fear that something the child has may be taken away. For example, an insecure child may feel that if her parents love her brother, there is less love for her. Jealousy can be a very destructive emotion. It can undermine a child's feeling of self-worth and she may feel guilty about feeling jealous.

What can parents do to deal with jealousy?

Be conscious of treating each child as an individual and valuing their different qualities. It's never too late to begin. Find ways to make each child feel special, give them each one-on-one time each day. Explain to them that love is magic. The more you give away, the more you have left to give away.

Talk about feelings, including jealousy. Allow your child the opportunity to explore these feelings and verbalise them. Continue reinforcing positive messages, and build your child's self-esteem. As a parent, try to be even-handed with your children. There may be more of an emotional connection with one, but you can always find qualities in all your children that you admire and love.

There will be times when one of your children behaves in a way that makes it difficult to like her. This does not mean that you will stop loving your child. These feelings are quite normal.

What can we do to foster our child's independence?

As a child moves through primary school towards puberty, there can be increasing conflict over her desires and the limits set by her parents. Try to make space for your child to assert her growing independence. Create positive opportunities for her individuality to be expressed. Give her more responsible tasks in the house. Encourage your child to participate more actively in adult conversation and share her views. Ask her for her opinion in family discussions.

How do we teach our children good decision-making skills?

A child should be gradually eased into the process of decision-making. You can invite her to participate in simple tasks such as who to invite to her birthday party, how to spend her pocket money, and what clothes to purchase. As she gets older, you can increase the amount of responsibility by offering a wider range of choices.

One of life's most vital skills is the capacity to solve problems. I believe there is a solution to every problem. I believe in the 'can do' philosophy. Your child needs to build up a bank of experience to draw on when she faces problems. The sooner you encourage her to come up with solutions for herself, the more confidence she will have in working out an answer to a problem.

Some parents feel they are doing their children a favour by solving problems for them.

It's very tempting, especially when you can see your child struggling with an issue, to jump in and save her. However, if you provide the solution, your child is not learning to deal with disappointment, conflict and frustration. Take the time to sit down with your child. Help her to solve her own problems by asking the right questions:

- 'What is the problem?'
- 'How do you feel about it?' (Help her to use words such as 'angry', 'frustrated', 'upset' and 'hurt'.)
- 'Why do you think it happened?'
- 'What can you do that will make you feel better?'
- 'How can you prevent this happening again?'

Let your child come up with possible solutions.

- 'Which solutions would you like to try?'
- Praise her for coming up with her own ideas.

Each time your child solves a problem successfully, her confidence grows. To enhance this skill you can include your child in some family discussions. Show her how to define a problem, brainstorm possible solutions, and then choose a line of action by assessing the options.

What do parents fear when their children start going to school?

Bullying has become the major problem in the school environment. We also witness shocking scenes of shooting sprees and violent behaviour. In some cases, children have even been sexually assaulted by their classmates.

Your child may be the bully or the victim of a bully. A child may have become a victim as a result of some physical aspect of her appearance that she has no control over, such as being short or having red hair. She may be socially isolated and a target for other children.

Bullies often prey on children with low self-esteem. They learn that the children who lack confidence are less likely to fight back. If your child has not shared her experiences of bullying with you, you can watch for signs that your child is not his usual self:

- He may be withdrawn.
- He may have unexplained injuries.
- He may express fears about going to school.
- He may have trouble sleeping.
- He may return from school with torn clothing.
- His school performance may deteriorate.

How can we help our child deal with bullying tactics?

It is of critical importance to teach our children how to deal with bullies. We need to encourage our child to stand up for himself instead of getting upset, crying and giving in to the bully. Engage your child in discussion and show him what the bully may get out of the interaction. He may be showing off to his peers or he may want to get attention due to his own low self-esteem. He may also be experiencing some troubles in his own life and bullying may be a way for him to express his feelings about this.

Make sure your child knows it is both acceptable and important to tell a teacher or parent about the bullying when it starts. An adult can support and empower your child, therefore removing the power from the bully. Explain that high emotions will only encourage the bully to continue the torment. Teach your child the value of 'cooling off' in order to gain control by counting, taking deep breaths, walking away, or talking to another friend. The key to fending off bullies is to build your child's self-esteem. This enables her to realise the problem lies with the bully and not herself.

When your child tells you, or implies, that he is being bullied at school, ask him two questions: What are the children doing to upset you? How does that make you feel?

Encourage him to get it off his chest by letting him know that you want to help. Let your child come up with possible solutions. These are some ways in which your child could respond to the bully. For example:

- Ignore the teasing or bullying.
- Make friends with other children for support.
- Teach your child to be assertive.
- Deflect the bullying with humour.
- Speak out, saying, 'Stop that, I don't like it'.
- Engaging friends to help him stand up to the bully.

By helping him come up with his own solutions, he regains the power that he has lost through being tormented. He feels better about himself and regains confidence. If the bullying continues, you should consider speaking to your child's teacher.

What do you do if your child is the aggressor?

This information may come to you via the teacher if it is serious, or possibly via another parent. Work out if there are any major issues in your child's life; any things which may be causing him to act like a bully. Clearly articulate that all forms of physical violence – pushing, shoving and hitting – are unacceptable. A child who bullies usually has low self-esteem and needs help. She may be acting out some conflict she is experiencing at home, or she may have some internal stress she is dealing with. Talk to your child and the teacher. If the behaviour continues, have your child assessed by a professional psychologist or the school counsellor.

How can we ensure that our children form positive friendships?

We all need friends – they play a vital role in our psychological health. As a child develops, her potential for friendships deepens. She learns about friendship) from a young age, by watching her parents and siblings, and through interacting with other children.

In primary school years, friendship waxes and wanes. There may be times when your child feels left out of a group, or feels let down by a friend. These experiences can be painful. Empathise with your child and discuss her feelings using the problem-solving skills discussed earlier in this chapter.

Encourage your child to make new friends, to invite them over to your home, and to include his friends in a wide spectrum of activities. There will be times when your child has, in your opinion, an undesirable friend. Rather than forbidding the friendship, allow him to discover the differences in values and home life, and discuss these with her. It is good for children to mix with a wide spectrum of friends. It helps them realise that people come from different backgrounds and cultures.

What is the best strategy for handling homework?

I believe homework has many benefits, including teaching a child how to study independently. Therefore, parents have an important role in helping their child develop effective homework routines. When your child comes home from school, make sure he has some time to relax and unwind. This does not necessarily mean watching TV, but it may include having afternoon tea and talking about the day.

Some children have a very busy schedule of afternoon activities, which may include sport, ballet, art, music or tutoring. Children have a long day at school and you need to be selective in your choice of extra activities. Maybe let them select two per semester so that they can try various activities but are not overburdened.

Decide whether homework will be done in the family living area or in the bedroom. Make sure there is a good table, a desk lamp and minimal distraction. If your child develops good homework habits in primary school he will adapt better in high school. The sooner he gets his homework finished, the sooner he can go out to play or watch television.

Should you help your child with homework?

The purpose of homework is to promote independent study. If your child is struggling, you may assist him. You may need to test him with his spelling or ask him to read you a story he has written. Don't give him the answers to homework problems; rather, help him find the answers for himself. Praise him for his efforts.

Some children find homework very difficult. The attention and encouragement a parent can give a child, therefore, can make a significant difference. As your child gets older, he will have projects that involve research. Show him how to look up information and encourage him to become an independent fact-finder.

Toolbox

- The best gift you can give your child is your undivided attention.
- Create family rules and explain them clearly to your child.
- Allow your child to help around the house. Give him regular chores to carry out.
- Decide how much pocket money your child should receive. This may vary with age. Discuss what he has to purchase with this money.
- Limit exposure to television and monitor the programs your child watches. Don't use the television as a babysitter.
- Discuss with your child when homework should be done, and create a calm environment in which he can do it.
- Discuss and enforce consequences of negative behaviour.
- Discuss family values with your child. Explain clearly which ones are important to your family.
- Let your children sort out their own fights with their siblings, unless someone is in danger of being hurt.
- Allow your child to explore all his feelings, including jealousy.
- Encourage your child's independence. Allow him to solve his own problems where possible.

chapter sixteen

Living Happily with Teenagers

KAREN, AN INTELLIGENT FIFTEEN-YEAR-OLD GIRL with excellent communication skills, is one of three children. In her formative years she was set insufficient limits by her parents, and was over-indulged. Her parents did not present a united front, so she soon learned that if one parent said 'no', the other would say 'yes'.

Karen was given anything that she wanted, yet she was very unhappy. At school, she mixed with the 'trendies' and rejected the girls who were as intelligent as her. Karen also reacted badly to discipline, both at home and at school. She started acting up at school and became increasingly withdrawn at home. She started mixing with children who were much older and was caught smoking marijuana. Her parents discovered that Karen had been lying to them for some time.

Fortunately, Karen was keen to receive help and was happy to have weekly therapy sessions. After talking with her, I soon realised that her parents, Diane and David, have always been supportive of her, and were not to blame for the things she had done. After seeing me weekly for six months, Karen handed me a list of the lessons she had learned from our therapy:

- Never lie to myself. It prevents me from taking responsibility for my actions.
- Don't lie to others. Remember, I only tell a lie when I am ashamed of what I did.

- ❖ Ask myself, 'Is this something I would be happy for my family and friends to know?' If the answer is 'no', then don't do it.
- ❖ It is okay to make mistakes, as long as I learn from them.
- ❖ Set a standard as to how I want to be treated by future boyfriends.
- ❖ Remember, I will be treated the way I expect to be treated.
- ❖ In future relationships, don't give of myself sexually unless I am sure that the boy loves me as much as I love him. I am too special to allow a boy to use me for his sexual gratification.
- ❖ Remember that it is the easiest thing in the world to lose our good reputation. but the hardest thing in the world to regain it.
- ❖ When choosing friends ask myself,'Do I respect this person? Does he/she respect me? Do I feel good about myself when I am in this person's company? Would I be proud to introduce this person as my friend?'
- ❖ Treat people the way I want to be treated. If someone is nasty to me, I won't be nasty back. Never lower myself to another person's standard. From now on, I promise I am going to expect to be treated as someone very special, because I am special.
- ❖ I am in charge of my life. I have choices, and taking responsibility for my choices empowers me.
- ❖ Don't say something behind someone's back that I would not want her to overhear.

During adolescence a teenager is faced with the task of learning how to become an independent person. In order to do this, she may need to rebel against the very people she loves most. She may need to break free from her family. On the journey towards discovering herself, her peer group becomes increasingly important to her.

This is a time when teenagers experiment, try out different roles, and search for answers to questions. In their attempt to cut the emotional ties to their parents, they are often filled with a sense of loss and emptiness.

Teenagers goes through a period of enormous growth and development. They experience physical changes in their bodies, hormonal changes that impact on their moods, and changes in personal and social expectations. Adolescence, therefore, is a time of instability, insecurity, restlessness and turmoil. It can be a difficult time for parents as well as for the teenager. However, it is a vital phase of transition from childhood to adulthood, a time of growth, independence and adventure.

Most parents dread the onset of adolescence, anticipating a difficult time. Does it have to be this way?

If parents understand the changes a teenager is experiencing, they can learn to make this a more positive, productive time.

Could you highlight some of the core areas of conflict during adolescence?

Problems arise over curfew times, coming home late, school performance, personal habits, untidy rooms, spending habits, choice of friends, drugs, alcohol, and communication issues.

Some parents do not cope well with the change. They are used to parenting children. As the needs of the adolescent change, parents need to adapt their style. Some overparent, others don't know how to set limits. This period can become a battleground where both sides are at war with each other – this is an emotionally devastating experience.

The aim is to keep lines of communication open and learn to listen to your teenager. Many adults may have forgotten their own experience of adolescence. I encourage them to get in touch with their own struggles at that stage of their life. Here are some tools to enable parents to do this. Think about your own family and ask yourself the following questions:

- Could you trust your parents to take care of your needs?
- Did you feel loved just for being you, not only for what you achieved?
- Did your parents make you feel unique and special?

- Did your parents encourage you to be your best, and explore your talents and interests?
- Did they set limits but also allow freedom?
- Were you given the support to do what you wanted?
- Did you feel you could turn to them for help if you got into trouble?
- Did they encourage you to solve your own problems and make independent decisions?
- Did they criticise your friends, clothes or music?
- Did they respect your ideas and take your opinions seriously?

As your children approach adolescence, take a look at yourself. Become the kind of parent you wish you had had. This is an opportunity not to blame your parents, but to acknowledge that we live in different times. We have much more information and understanding at our disposal to give us insight into adolescence. At the same time, our teenagers face a much more demanding, stressful and complex world than we did.

In what way is a teenager's world different?

There are more pressures on adolescents to perform academically because consequences are more significant in terms of their long-term careers. There are many more opportunities and choices, which is wonderful, but it can be very confusing also.

It is a time of ambiguity. On the one hand, teenagers push towards independence and freedom, but on the other hand they want to be looked after when things go wrong. It is very tempting to get into the 'I told you so' syndrome if things go wrong, instead of being non-judgmental. I teach parents and teenagers to try to communicate, especially when things go wrong. They need to stop blaming each other. Threats and accusations have no benefit other than to hurt the other person. Retreating into sullen silence is also counterproductive.

Adolescents attack parents when they feel insecure. We must resist the temptation to attack back.

How do we get our teenagers to respect us?

Another dead end is to focus on the issue of respect. This drives the parent and adolescent even further apart. Parents must earn respect; it is not their automatic right. Respect is a mutual energy exchange, so it is imperative that you lead by example. Model respect in the way you treat your adolescent and others around you. Don't yell, or use abusive language or put-downs. Never negate her feelings, and be available to listen whenever she wants to talk. You will earn respect by acting respectfully.

How do we enforce rules and directions?

Be clear about the non-negotiable rules. Understand that you cannot treat your teenager the way you do pre-schoolers. It is extremely difficult and often counterproductive to forbid him to see friends, to ground him or to forbid alcohol, although you could certainly forbid him to drink-drive. Stress that if he does, he will forfeit use of the car for two weeks.

Establish as few rules as possible and only set limits you have the power to enforce. Work out the non-negotiable rules and discuss them with your teenager. If your teenager feels he has played a part in setting the rules and coming up with solutions, he will be far more likely to agree to stick to them. For example, if you forbid smoking entirely, you encourage devious behaviour. If you forbid smoking at home, you will be able to monitor that behaviour in your home. Decide what household chores your teenager is responsible for. Insist that school work is done on time. Keep interference in your adolescent's life to a minimum.

How much freedom do we give teenagers?

Expect them to express their individuality and reserve the negatives or criticisms for really important issues. Encourage your teenager to develop her own taste in clothing, arrange her room the way she wants and choose her own friends. The teenage years are about self-exploration and self-expression. Your teenager may appear with torn jeans, spiked hair and an earring in her nose. Allow her to rebel against the establishment if she chooses; to express her individuality. You may not like the dreadlocks and the scruffy look, but look at the big picture. Don't be afraid. She is finding out about who she is and where she fits into this diverse and daunting world. Remember also that you are focusing on her external appearance. All that really matters is what's going on inside the mind and soul of your teen. Focus your energies on nurturing that instead. If you attempt to suppress self-expression, your teenager will feel forced to rebel, or suppress her emotions to avoid the criticism.

Understand that an adolescent has a need for, and a right to, privacy. On no account should you attempt to pry into her life either by interrogation, reading her diary, snooping in her room or listening to private phone conversations. Your adolescent is entitled to a private and independent life.

Many mothers go into their teenager's rooms and 'accidentally' discover things. This will only create more problems. Your teenager will not trust you and you run the risk of alienating her at a time when she needs background parental support the most. Make your teenager responsible for tidying her own room. Let her live in a mess if she chooses. Close the door. Respect her privacy.

Parents like to think they can choose their teenager's friends, or steer them in the direction of the 'right' kinds of friends. A teenager is fiercely protective of his friends, who often seem like the only people on his side. We all surround ourselves with people we can relate to and connect with, and who make us feel that we are okay as we are. Your teenager is no different.

Focus your energy on your teenager, not on the company she keeps. Give your attention to things you can actually influence, such as your teenager's self-esteem. Boost your teen's feelings about herself, rather than criticising his friends which will have the opposite effect. If you continue to condemn your teenager's friends, you will alienate her further. She will spend as much time as possible with the very people you want her to stay away from.

How do we protect our teenager from making mistakes?

While you are giving your teenager increasing freedom, you can also make sure she understands the consequences of inappropriate behaviour. It may be tempting to solve your teenager's problems and protect her from potential hardship. The best way for her to learn, however, is by her own experience. We are often keen to rescue our children, but they learn quicker by trial and error, as long as they are not in physical danger. Trust yourself as a parent. Know that if you raised your child well, the foundations are there.

How else can we work towards a harmonious relationship with our teenager?

Always provide a 'why' when saying 'no' to your teenager. She deserves an explanation. It may prevent a full-blown argument later. When you say no or turn her down, provide an alternative option or a compromise. This enables her to feel that she is walking away with something, and that she hasn't 'lost' to Mum and Dad again.

It may be appropriate to have a family meeting every few weeks. This can be done informally. This gives parents an opportunity to listen to their teenagers and vice versa. If a particular issue is causing both you and your teenager some heartache, you may say something like, 'We need a win–win situation here, what do you suggest we could do or change to make sure that neither of us continues to feel unhappy about this?'

Like anyone else, no teenager likes to have rules imposed on her, or decisions made for her, without prior discussion. We all know how it feels to be told what to do. Involve your teenager in the decision-making process. At this time, address any sticky issues, talk them through rationally and come up with solutions together. Be fair and open to suggestions. Be prepared to compromise. Ask your teenager her opinion. This will boost her self-esteem and make her feel mature and respected.

One of the frustrating things about teenagers is that they often seem to waste a lot of time. We race around doing our jobs, shopping, household chores and they appear to spend a lot of time hanging out.

Teenagers do spend a lot of time watching television, listening to music, having long telephone conversations with friends, and daydreaming. These activities are an integral part of the stage of adolescence.

A teenager can be moody, and often the moods are caused by nothing in particular. In fact, the worst thing you can do is keep asking 'What's wrong?' Allow her the space to have her highs and lows. The moodiness is often hormonal or a result of relationship issues with her peer group.

This is the time for teens to experiment with relationships, test their independence and try some of the activities that belong in the adult domain. The more we nag them, the more defensive they become. If you interrogate them, they will either withdraw or go off in a huff.

PRESENT A UNITED FRONT TO YOUR CHILDREN

IF YOU AND YOUR PARTNER DISAGREE ON WHAT IS ALLOWED AND WHAT IS FORBIDDEN, YOU ARE CREATING CONFUSION AND INSTABILITY FOR YOUR CHILD, AND SETTING THEM TO PLAY ONE PARENT AGAINST THE OTHER. IT IS LIKE WORKING FOR TWO BOSSES WHO HAVE DIFFERENT VIEWS ON HOW YOU SHOULD DO YOUR WORK!

So what is the best way to handle these reactions?
Keep the channels of communication open. Give empathy, not judgement, when she shares her feelings. Listen with an open mind and avoid being critical.

Provide as much positive feedback and praise as you can. Don't, however, be insincere with your praise. If you are, your teen will not respect your opinion. Do not dismiss any of your teenager's feelings as being 'silly teenage issues' that she'll grow out of. Let her know that you respect and acknowledge her feelings. She will then become more relaxed about sharing her experiences with you.

One of the big issues I remember with my teenagers was what time to set their curfew and how many nights they should be allowed to go out a week. What is the best way to deal with the issue of curfews?
Curfew times will change as the teen matures. You may start out with a ten pm curfew for thirteen-year-olds and then gradually extend the time allowed out. Resist being drawn into a comparison conversation with your teenager about what her friends are doing. Make your limits clear, and establish a protocol for emergencies. For example, she must call you if she is delayed. She will test the limits, however, and you need to be prepared to implement the consequences.

When I was about fifteen years old, my parents made it clear that if I was ever in a sticky situation I could call them at any time of the night. They would pick me up from anywhere with no questions asked. They also told me that if I needed a scapegoat to get out of any situation, such as being offered drugs, I could 'blame' my parents. For example, I could say, 'Sorry I have to go, my parents are being difficult at the moment, they've restricted my curfew'. My parents were quite generous with this. By giving me a way out, I did not have to look weak in front of my peers.

How should we respond to their friends?

Don't judge your teenager's friends. As long as they include and accept her, make them feel welcome. Always encourage your children to bring friends home. Have a supply of snack food so that you can be hospitable to your teenager's friends. Get to know them. Remember their names and make them feel welcome.

How should we deal with the issue of money?

Decide how much financial support you are prepared to give your teenager. You may have a set allowance. Discuss what the allowance should cover. For example, entertainment, transport, snacks away from home and gifts for her friends.

You can start with a certain amount when she is twelve or thirteen years old, and gradually increase this as she gets older. You may give her an opportunity to earn more by doing extra chores such as washing the car or mowing the lawn, but basic help around the house should not be linked to financial reward.

By the age of fifteen, your teen is old enough to get a part-time job and earn her own money to supplement her allowance. I believe strongly in part-time jobs, as they foster independence. Teach your teenager how to budget and save. Start her off with positive spending patterns and financial management skills, and she will be financially stable for the rest of her life. Resist the temptation to give your teenager constant handouts. It is not teaching her how the real world fluctuates.

I agree; my kids had part-time jobs. In the six years that my son was a medical student he coached tennis, sold ice cream, worked in a real estate office and tutored high school students. I believe these jobs gave him experience in handling a wide range of situations, as well as financial independence, and the ability to make choices.

How can we develop decision making skills in our teenagers?

I believe one of the main roles of parents is to develop the decision-making skills in their teenagers. Let your teenager practice making decisions. Give her a chance to explore options and try out situations. There is no substitute for first-hand experience and the practise of making independent choices, even if she makes mistakes.

Allow her to decide what clothes to purchase, what courses to take at school, how she spends her own money. If she asks your advice, act as a consultant but still allow her to make the final decision. Be available without rescuing her. This will give her confidence. Make your motto, 'Discuss issues, don't tell her what to do'.

Are there any other problems we should be aware of?

Adolescence brings with it a multitude of challenges. As your teenager goes through physical changes, she may need to learn to cope with pimples, acne, weight problems and a negative self-image. Help your teen feel good about herself. Be observant, especially with girls and their diet. Eating disorders are very prevalent. Often girls will hide problems for as long as they can. If you suspect something is wrong, encourage your teenager to share the problem. Get expert advice as early as possible.

Social problems may also occur at this stage. Being popular and part of the peer group is important in establishing your teenager's identity. If you notice her spending excessive time alone, not going out much or connecting less with friends, try to find out what is happening. Watch out for depression. Learn to tell the difference between a low mood, which may only be around for a few days, and signs of a depression. Depression or radical changes in behaviour may be a symptom of drug use.

How do we handle the issue of drugs with our teenagers?

It is extremely difficult to forbid your teenagers to experiment with drugs, especially marijuana. It will only increase their desire to find out for themselves. They will want to know what all the fuss is about. Education is the best option. Talk about drugs freely, introduce open discussions around the dinner table and with their friends, leave articles or books about the harmful effects of drugs and smoking lying around. The less 'taboo' the drugs sound, the less your teen will want to try them. Teens are intelligent; if they have knowledge and understanding of important issues, it won't necessarily stop them experimenting, but they will know why it isn't safe to partake. They will then feel safer making decisions that are different from those of their peers.

Look for problems before they reach too far down the track. Let your teenager know that you trust him. Try to be the parent you wished you had had. Here is an example where parents successfully communicated with their son about drug issues.

JENNIFER AND RICHARD WANTED ADVICE about their sixteen-year-old son, Michael, whom they had realised was smoking marijuana. When cleaning his room one day Jennifer had found a box under his bed containing six joints. There had been no changes in Michael's behaviour, his school work had not deteriorated, his behaviour was not secretive, his mood had not altered, and there was no money missing.

Although Richard and I are aware that a large proportion of sixteen-year-olds has tried drugs, we had to decide how we would handle the situation. We knew that if we mishandled it, it could close the door to the good relationship and open communication we felt we had with Michael.

Jennifer and Richard remembered their own teenage years; being cross-examined by parents regarding where they were going, whom they were meeting, and when they would be home. They remembered the resentment and anger they had often felt whenever they had not met parental expectations, and were forced to listen to parental 'lectures'.

We discussed their feelings about Michael smoking marijuana. They were not shocked, nor were they angry. They did not feel that Michael had betrayed their trust. Nonetheless they were concerned, and wanted to let Michael know that they did not condone it, and to calmly point out certain facts for Michael to think about:

- It was illegal.
- If he smoked or was caught with it at school, he could be suspended.
- Whoever was selling him the drugs may eventually try to persuade him to try some harder drug.

Before sitting down with Michael, I suggested that they get information from CEIDA (the Centre for Education and Information on Drugs and Alcohol). 'We knew frequent use of marijuana could affect his energy and drive, interest in other things, and motivation, and long-term use could decrease his concentration and memory, which in turn could affect his learning ability.'

It would be of no use forbidding Michael to ever smoke marijuana, but it was essential that they ask him to think carefully about what they had discussed, and to read the relevant information so that any decision he made would be a responsible one, based on knowledge.

How do we handle school performance?

When it comes to performance and achievement at school, the worst thing you can do is nag your child to study. I believe you should state your expectations. It may be simply that you expect your child to do her best according to her potential and be diligent about handing assignments in on time. This is her responsibility.

When her school report arrives, if she has performed well, give positive feedback. If she has underachieved or has been negligent, talk it through with her rather than punish her. Find out where the problems are. There may be problems in other areas of her life that are affecting her ability to concentrate. Discuss these and give your teenager the opportunity to improve before taking punitive measures. Find other areas that may offer her a chance to shine; perhaps sport, music, art or drama. Give her an opportunity to discover her talents in a broad range of areas. Not everyone is an academic achiever.

How can we support our teenager during exam time?

For a lot of teens, studying is difficult, and they may find that their minds go blank in exams. First of all, make sure your teen actually knows how to study. There is a skill involved. Offer to send her to a study-skills workshop. It will help to remove any fears she has, and she will discover how easy it is to learn.

Talk to your teen about preparing a study timetable. Ask to assist with it or see it, so that you can be supportive and prepare dinner or a 'quiet' house at the appropriate times. Get involved in an easy-going, interested, relaxed kind of way.

Accept that she may get stressed or irritable around this time. Just go with the flow, rather than trying to change her behaviour at this important time. If you observe that she doesn't handle pressure very well, take steps to help her with this. Be as supportive as possible. Do some research; find some courses or tutors who can help her cope with the pressures of school work and study.

What's the best way to resolve conflicts in general?

As with all conflict, both teenager and parents must realise that there are two sides to every argument. Each side needs to own their contribution to the conflict. Instead of blaming, yelling and threatening, sit down and invite your adolescent to share her side of the story. Try to look at the problem from her perspective. Give her your undivided attention. State your feelings. Speak using 'I' statements. For example, 'I am upset', or 'I feel anxious'. Share your concern and feelings.

Aim to listen to each other. Try to come to a win–win solution where both parties walk away happy. Show your teenager that you respect and understand her position. Keep the channels open. If she retreats into silence, be the first to break the silence and make every effort to keep talking. The continued connection is needed to reach resolution.

Whenever you get into an argument with your teen, or come across a tricky issue, take a second consider your outcome. Pinpoint exactly what it is that you want to achieve. Get a picture in your mind of the end result of this discussion. Ensure that all your communication supports that outcome. There are times when an outcome is non-negotiable. In this situation, you would need to stand your ground. Choose your outcome and keep it in mind constantly.

Is there anything a parent should not do during an argument?

Don't force your teenager to apologise as a mark of respect to your parental authority. If you insist on an apology, you may further damage the relationship. The teenager may feel humiliated, frustrated and angry.

There are times when people who are emotionally close quarrel and say hurtful things. Be ready to forgive your teenager without waiting for the big apology. Keep sharing and keep on trying to understand each other. Stay focused on a specific area of conflict. When one is upset, it is tempting to bring other issues into the argument. This confuses the issue. Restrict discussion to one area of conflict.

Don't take your teen's behaviour personally. Anything that she says is not about you as a parent. It's about how your teen feels about herself. Sadness is often expressed as anger first. She is projecting her fears and insecurities onto you because you are the closest person to her and so she feels relatively safe doing so. Ironically, this is an honour.

How do we approach sexual issues with teens?

It is impossible to give hard and fast rules regarding what is appropriate, but there are a few guidelines that may help navigate this thorny issue. First of all, know that sexual activity will vary from teen to teen, depending on physical maturity, peer group and influence of their family and school culture. Encourage open discussion about sex with your teenager. Clarify your own views. You are entitled to say, 'We believe that sexual intercourse is best experienced in a loving relationship.' Be clear about your values.

Your teen may or may not experiment with casual sex. Whatever the case, it is important to give her information about sexuality, contraception and protection. Do not assume she knows it all or that the school provides this information. Accept that your teen will probably not discuss her sexual experiences with you. Explain that she does not have to do things just because all her friends may be doing it. The media, romantic movies and the Internet give the impression that everyone is having sex all the time.

Give your teen an understanding of the role of sex in a relationship. In the early teenage years, teenagers are self-absorbed. Your teenager may have a strong sex drive and be more interested in the satisfaction of her needs than in a relationship. Explain these issues to your teenager, and encourage her to approach her sexuality with responsibility. If a teen waits until she has the emotional maturity to handle a full sexual relationship, she may save herself a lot of emotional insecurity. Every family will have their own values and attitudes to sex, nudity and sexual expression. Clarify yours. Your teen will be very aware of how you conduct your life. Don't be hypocritical.

What are the most valuable general tips for parents of teenagers?

Get to know your teenager like a friend without relinquishing your role as a parent. Some parents try to be 'cool' and fit in with their teen. This, ironically, serves to alienate her further. Your teenager has to have boundaries. It is hard for her to know where she stands in most situations at this time. There is confusion with the opposite sex, with fashion sense, with academic potential, and with career prospects. Your teen needs to know where she stands with her parents.

Discuss the concept of boundaries. Ask her what her boundaries are, what makes her angry or frustrated. Make a conscious effort to respect those boundaries. Your teen will feel 'heard', respected, and happy that someone cares enough to ask her what matters to her. Let her know what your boundaries are. Choose your three top ones. Make sure they are realistic, simple and achievable.

Toolbox

- ✤ Respect your adolescent as an individual.
- ✤ Be curious about her opinions.
- ✤ Focus on the positive.
- ✤ Resist being critical when it comes to clothes, friends or taste in music. Your teenager's choices are supposed to be different from yours.
- ✤ Give your teenager space and distance, but make sure she knows you're there if she needs you.
- ✤ Be clear about her responsibilities. Give her privileges in return for fulfilled responsibilities. This changes as she gets older. Give her the right to choose. If she doesn't fulfil her responsibilities, she loses the privilege.
- ✤ Be consistent. Set few rules, but ones you can enforce.
- ✤ Be prepared for challenges, rebellion and testing the limits. This is the journey of adolescence.
- ✤ Discuss sex, drugs, smoking and alcohol with her. Provide information and open discussion.
- ✤ Discuss financial support. Encourage her to get a part-time job and to save.

chapter seventeen

Impact of Separation and Divorce on Children

EVERY YEAR, MORE THAN 50,000 children in Australia are affected by the divorce of their parents. The early 1970s saw a marked increase in the rate of divorce, so we have now had the time span of a generation to assess the effects of divorce on those children, now adults.

Initially, many people, including psychologists, believed that divorce was no big deal for kids; they would coast through the difficult times, recover and bounce back. However, this is not what happened. Therapist Judith Wallerstein, in her book *The Unexpected Legacy of Divorce*, argues that 'the harm caused by divorce is grave and longer lasting than we suspected'.

Wallerstein has spent three decades carrying out in-depth interviews with children of divorce. She discovered that children take a long time to get over divorce. They often suffer learning disabilities, depression, and other psychological problems. The most disturbing finding was that when children reach maturity, they often struggle to form their own adult relationships. There is a 'sleeper' effect of divorce, with some aspects taking years to reveal themselves. Susie has spent many years working with families going through separation and divorce.

Should a couple stay together for better or for worse, considering the damage divorce has on children?

Definitely not. When one considers the financial, physical and emotional stresses of going through a divorce, I cannot believe any parents divorce without deep consideration. In addition, there are many families where there is physical or emotional abuse, substance addiction or other severe pathologies. There is no doubt that some marriages cannot be sustained.

Children also suffer when they are living in an atmosphere of continual conflict, quarrels and intense hostility, which may include physical or verbal abuse. This does not provide them with a positive model for marriage or relationships. Certain couples may still care about each other and be prepared to invest in learning skills to get along more effectively. But I wouldn't say that staying in a very unhappy marriage is the solution. I believe there are ways of getting divorced that can minimise the harmful effects on children.

Could you outline some of these ways?

Parents should be civil to each other. Getting divorced is a time of high emotion, but giving in to anger, violence and yelling makes things worse. Often if one partner has been left, he may want to punish the other as a form of revenge. This can take the form of withholding financial support. Another area where couples try to get even or hurt each other is by denying access to the children, or criticising the other parent in front of the children. All of these actions cause damage to them.

When parents come to me for divorce counselling, I tell them from the beginning that I work for the children, fighting for their rights. To minimise the adverse effects of the divorce, I make parents aware that their hostility and anger towards each other can cause long-lasting emotional problems for their children. The adults have their lawyers to fight for their financial well-being; the children have me to fight for their emotional well-being. I can be very fierce with adults who are

behaving badly, as my goal is to minimise the harmful impact on the children. In the long term, parents will benefit as well.

The greatest mistake parents make when they are going through separation or divorce is to criticise each other to their children. I explain to parents that their child is made up of one half mother and one half father. When either parent criticises each other, the child feels as if half of them is being criticised. This is exacerbated in a moment of anger at the child, when one parent says to their child, 'You are just like your mother/father.' When a parent aims an arrow at their spouse via their child, it lodges in the heart of their child.

Look at divorce through a child's eyes. As it is happening, he probably feels as if though his whole world is falling apart. He is scared, becoming anxious about what the future holds. Who will look after me? Where will I live? Will I have to leave my school and friends?

The way to minimise these fears is to take control. Explain to your children, 'You don't have to worry where you are going to live. We both love you and will take care of your needs'. Reassure them. Problems arise when parents are weak and indecisive. Explain to your children that some things will change but you will make sure everything is taken care of. Children need structure, routine and your confidence that you will cope as well.

What else can we do to reduce the negative impact on our children?

Both mother and father should try to remain strong in front of their children. Your child will cope far better if she sees that you are coping. She needs your strength. The child should not feel she is suddenly responsible for her parent's emotional well-being. Even if you are feeling emotionally vulnerable, tearful, insecure and unhappy – act strong. Put on the act of your life and find other sources of support. Get a therapist, go to a group, use a friend, but do not rely on your child for support.

Wherever possible, maintain your children's schedule of activities. If you can, stay in the same house for as long as possible. Keep your children in the same school, and keep their routines consistent. Provide as much continuity as you can. Go to both sets of grandparents and family and ask them to maintain contact with the children, as they will need it more than ever.

If you start searching for a new relationship, don't go out every night leaving your children at home. Initially, try to go out when your partner has access, so that you do not diminish your time with your children.

NEVER ARGUE WITHIN EARSHOT OF YOUR CHILDREN

IT IS TRAUMATIC FOR CHILDREN TO HEAR THEIR PARENTS FIGHT. IT MAKES THEM FEEL VERY INSECURE. IF YOU AND YOUR PARTNER NEED TO DISCUSS AN ISSUE, GO TO ANOTHER ROOM AND SHUT THE DOOR. EVEN BETTER, WAIT UNTIL THEY ARE NOT AROUND.

What is the best way to tell children that you are separating?

The best way is to tell the children altogether. Explain to them that you are very sad, that you have tried hard to work things out, but you both feel the best solution is to separate. Don't blame the other parent, even if the decision was not yours. Don't give them false hopes. Couples who separate and come together again several times create a rollercoaster ride for the children. They keep hoping the divorce is a nightmare that will end.

Make sure your children know that the divorce is not their fault. Children often blame themselves and think there is something they should have done to prevent the divorce. Talk to your children about their feelings. Once they have words that fit their emotions they can articulate their feelings. Sharing their emotions and knowing that you understand how they feel is very helpful.

How much should you tell your children about the reasons for getting divorced?

I believe it depends on a child's age and the circumstances. I don't believe any purpose can by served by discussing extra-marital affairs with the children. I encourage couples who are in another relationship to introduce that new person to their children only several weeks after the separation.

Give age-appropriate explanations to the child. Don't tell your child things with the express purpose of getting them to dislike their other parent. They will be much happier if they can continue to love their other parent without feeling guilty. The long-term effects of separating your child from the other parent can be severe and children take a long time to recover from divorce. However, by understanding the impact of your divorce on them, you can minimise its damage.

Is there any age at which children cope better?

There is no perfect age for children but young children and teenagers are probably more vulnerable. Toddlers and young children miss their other parent and find the concept of divorce difficult to understand. They interpret the loss of one parent as abandonment. Adolescents are going through enormous emotional, physical and psychological changes anyway. Divorce compounds the effects of these changes.

I have heard that for the child, divorce can be more traumatic than the death of a parent. Is this true?

I don't believe so, assuming that the non-custodial parent continues to have a loving relationship with the child, including frequent regular contact. However, divorce in the eyes of a child involves choice. Children may feel angry because you have chosen to break up their family. If you can conduct your divorce amicably, however, then it is nowhere near as hard for the children. Parents should behave in a way that gives permission to their children to love both parents without feeling guilty or

disloyal to either. They also need their pain and sadness acknowledged.

ALAN, NOW FORTY, WAS EIGHT when his parents separated. He is now married with two sons, aged nine and eleven. 'When my dad first left, I convinced myself he had gone on an extended holiday and that he was coming back. When I was about ten, Mum explained that they were getting divorced, and he wasn't coming back. In fact, he had left town.

I missed having a dad watch me play football and cricket. It was hard growing up without a father. Even when I was younger, Dad wasn't home much and did not play an active role in our lives. My grandfather and uncle were very good to me, and in many ways they acted as surrogate fathers. This compensated for Dad's absence. My mum, sister and I were very close, and I certainly wasn't deprived of love.

When I married, I decided I would do anything to keep my marriage together and avoid divorce. I now have two sons of my own, and I make sure that I spend a lot of time with them. Up until I was in my mid-twenties, I hated my father. By the time I was thirty and a father myself, I realised there was no mileage in being angry with him. We now see and talk to each other when he's in town, but I have no expectations of him. My grandfather was my male role model and from him I learnt about love, care, generosity, and character.

Gina, Alan's sister, was ten when her parents got divorced. Now forty-two, she has two daughters, aged thirteen and fifteen, and has been married for twenty years. I asked her about the impact of divorce on her life and her attitude. 'When my dad left, I didn't miss him much as we were never close. He wasn't around much when we were little and I never saw my parents argue. For the next ten years, my mum, my younger brother and I were a great team. We did everything together and we were very close. I had grandparents and uncles who filled the gap in our lives. My mother never said anything negative about my father, and so I still have a reasonable relationship with him.

The fact that Mum got divorced made me very conscious of choosing

a partner carefully. I didn't want to make a mistake. Although I was young when I married, twenty-two, I went out with my husband for four years and I felt confident about the relationship when we married. Moreover, having seen Mum cope well as a single parent, I would never put up with bad behaviour in my marriage.

'My husband knows what my values and standards are. I've made it clear to him that if he is unfaithful, there will be no second chance. As it happens, we have a really good marriage.

How do you decide which parent the children should live with, or is it better to share custody?

Parents need to make these decisions for the children, especially children under twelve. Children should not have to choose. This makes them feel guilty, no matter which parent they choose to live with. Make sure your children get to see both parents. Depending on your circumstances, some families choose to have children living partially in one home, and partially in the other. Or they could live with one parent and spend every second weekend with the other.

I believe that it is confusing to have children live in two places. It's important that they have a place that feels like home. This provides security, continuity and comfort. It can be very disorientating for children to do the 'move around' dance, packing up all their goods and chattels every few weeks or so. Then there is the drama of schoolbooks left behind, and clothes left at the other home.

When making these decisions, many factors need to be considered. They may include whether both parents work, suitability of accommodation, finances, and which parent has a closer and more open relationship with the children. There is no right or wrong answer. Some children find living in two homes difficult. Others want to spend equal time with both parents. Whatever the arrangement, there needs to be really good communication between parents. Messages should not be sent

via the children. If the children are unhappy with the chosen arrangements, then it will be necessary to re-evaluate them.

I prefer the arrangement of one residence with alternate weekends spent with the other parent. Children may choose to have dinner one night a week with the parent they are not living with. This helps provide the children with security, stability, continuity and comfort.

I saw a fourteen year-old-girl in therapy recently. She said the two most difficult things regarding her parents' divorce were the way her parents argued and yelled at each other, and sleeping at her dad's place on alternate weekends and one day during the week. She said that if she was wearing summer clothes and it suddenly turned cold, she didn't have warm clothes to change into. The logistics of moving from place to place became quite complicated.

Together, we came up with a solution for each situation. When her parents argued, I suggested she say to them in a firm voice, 'Mum, Dad, you are hurting me more than you are hurting each other'. This made her feel empowered. She also decided to keep some spare clothes at her dad's place in case the weather changed.

GIVE YOUR CHILD SPECIAL TIME

SPEND HALF AN HOUR OF SPECIAL TIME WITH YOUR CHILD AT LEAST THREE TIMES A WEEK. YOU SHOULD NOT BE DISTURBED, EVEN BY PHONE CALLS. LET HER CHOOSE A GAME OR ACTIVITY THAT ALLOWS THE TWO OF YOU TO INTERACT IN AN ENJOYABLE WAY

Often the anger and conflict escalates after separation. How do we handle this?

If you have children, especially young children, chances are you will have many years of contact with your partner. If there is still

an enormous amount of tension and hostility, some sessions of counselling can help you co-parent your children.

In my opinion, divorce counselling should be compulsory. This will help both partners deal with their emotions and prevent them from being destructive to each other and their children. Children become upset when you so much as hang up on your partner. When you argue in front of your children, you change who they are – by exposing them to verbal abuse, you eat away at their self-esteem. Children are sensitive, intuitive and vulnerable. Respect their feelings.

When we do start dating, and how soon can we introduce our children to new partners?

I would not rush to involve the children in your new relationships until you know that that person is going to become an ongoing part of your life. Make sure you spend one-on-one time with each of your children and give them space and time to adjust to all the changes in their lives. It would be very confusing for young children to cope with different partners in the place of their missing parent very soon after separation. Be patient in this area of your life.

What are other areas to consider?

Parents should not use children to carry messages to the other parent. This makes the child the piggie in the middle. Don't cross-examine your children about their experiences with the other parent unless you suspect negative issues such as neglect or abuse.

Be watchful and aware but don't interrogate the child. How children survive divorce is largely determined by the way parents choose to conduct the divorce. Since most children live with their mother post-divorce, the mother must look after herself so that she can be a strong and dependable parent. As Wallerstein says, 'Divorce is not more normal just because more people are touched by it'.

Children will never find divorce easy. Many children carry a big wish in their heart that their parents will reconcile, even if this wish is irrational and against all evidence. Sometimes the remarriage of one of the parents can be very traumatic, as it finally kills the dream of parents reconciling.

When one parent leaves, a child may experience tremendous rejection. This can reduce feelings of self-worth. They may think 'If he loved me he would not have left', or 'If I was better, he would spend more time with me'. As children get older they can learn to cope with their feelings of loss and forgive their parents for making them unhappy.

Children adjust to divorce more easily if both partners are an integral part of their lives. They need harmony between parents, and they need to be loved and respected by both parents. Both parents should attend school meetings and functions.

Children should have free access to both parents. They should be permitted to phone or see either parent without feeling that they would upset the other. Children should not have to choose between them. They need permission to love and connect with both.

What if one parent lives far away?

One parent can be good enough. Accept that your children may go through a period of missing their absent parent. There may be tears, sadness and grieving. Allow them these feelings and let them know that you are there to help.

However, encourage as much contact as possible. Children can e-mail, send pictures, mail copies of school reports and make phone calls. Set up a regular time each day or each week to call. All you can do is sympathise with your child if your ex-spouse does not maintain contact with your child. You could call and encourage him to make regular contact but there may be times you can't make it happen.

How do we ensure that the other parent is establishing similar rules when the child is spending time with him?
It may be necessary to sit down with a therapist or mediator to work out a consistent set of rules and consequences that will apply wherever the child is spending time. This may need to include bedtime, homework issues, how much television time and what kind of snacks they are allowed. If children have a different set of rules in each home they feel confused. As a parent, don't give in on issues out of guilt.

Some children do not express any dramatic emotions at the time of separation – does this mean they are coping well?
It may, but it could also be that the child is suppressing his emotions. When he sees one of his parents upset he may fear that exposing his emotions will only upset that parent more. Hidden feelings will increase anxiety, and may only show themselves at a later time when the child feels it is safer to reveal his feelings. Suppressed emotions can also show up in a decline in school performance, withdrawal and depression. If you see any signs of negative behaviour, talk to your child and, if necessary, take him to see a therapist.

What should we tell the school or teacher about the divorce?
I would definitely let the school know about changes in the family. They will provide support and encouragement during this time. A teacher will also then be alert to any changes in the child's performance and behaviour. Schools usually stay in touch with both parents separately.

I've taught children and I'm amazed at what they do share with teachers they trust.
Some schools also have a school psychologist who can be briefed if there is a difficult situation. Here are some of the dynamics that arise once parents have split up. If you are aware of these possibilities, you can act with caution.

Toolbox

- When one parent criticises or speaks badly about the other, be aware that you are hurting your child more than each other.
- Children experience loss and rejection when their parents divorce. Children's behaviour may deteriorate as a result of the pain they are experiencing. If you are a non-custodial parent, take care not to lose contact with your children post-divorce. This could lead to long-term detrimental effects.
- Don't be a Santa Claus parent and try to outdo the other parent in terms of treats in order to win your child's love. You can't buy love, you have to earn it.
- Divorce can be very traumatic for children no matter what their age. Be aware of their pain and, if possible, arrange counselling sessions to help them through this time.
- Try to stay strong in front of your children. They will feel more secure.
- Try to arrange for them to live in one place with plenty of access to the other parent.
- When you start seeing other people, don't go out every night and leave them with babysitters.
- Don't send messages to the other parent via the child.

chapter eighteen

Blended Families and Step-Parenting: Getting It Right

I SAW A COUPLE THAT had created a blended family. He had two teenage daughters; she had one teenage daughter and an eleven-year-old son. His household rules had been very different from the ones in her home. Fights developed between the couple, both feeling very protective of their own children. The arguments among the children caused chaos in the house.

I saw the parents first without the children, so that we could agree on rules for the home, and so that they could present a united front to the children. Once they had found compromises that suited both of them, they invited their children to the session. At the first session, they told the children that they had agreed on some rules that would help them all enjoy a peaceful home.

They were united in stating that the children did not have to love each other, but they did have to speak nicely to each other. This meant they had to watch their tone of voice, and had to put a stop to rude and bad-tempered responses. It was then the children's turn to air their grievances. It was important that the parents listened carefully to these, to let all the children know that their opinions mattered.

In future sessions, we discussed the common goal of family harmony, and brainstormed ideas. We decided on further rules and, with the children, worked out consequences for breaking the rules. I stressed to the parents that it was vital that the consequences be enforced.

The family soon learned how to resolve their conflicts, and created an atmosphere where every member of the family felt listened to and their feelings understood. There was then less need to express anger outside therapy. I also helped the family improve their communication skills and increase respect among family members. Within two months there was a tremendous improvement in the atmosphere in their home.

One of the consequences of our currently high divorce rate is that more and more people are having another go at marriage. The number of second marriages is increasing rapidly. Many of these marriages suffer a similar fate to first marriages, but for different reasons.

The biggest challenge facing parents who remarry is working out how to combine two families. Blended families are very different from a traditional family. Understanding the issues and acquiring coping skills can ease what may be a bumpy ride.

Blended families take many different forms. Your children may be toddlers, primary age or teenagers. Your partner's children may be of a similar age or an entirely different age. You and your partner may add new children to the existing family.

The way in which you put these two families together depends on all these variables. The younger the children, the more hands-on the parenting by the step-parent needs to be. Another variable is the amount of time your children and/or stepchildren spend with you and your partner. All these possible configurations represent a minefield of opportunities for explosions, arguments and heartache. An optimistic attitude combined with awareness and skills can, however, provide the basis for a complex yet rewarding family life.

What are the first steps towards creating harmony and happiness in a blended family?

Ideally, all the children should experience a sense of belonging. They need to feel that their emotions are respected and that their parents listen to their needs. Create some new rituals and traditions that belong to the new blended family. This can enhance the feeling of belonging together. Birthdays and special occasions can be an opportunity to reward each child and give special attention. Involve them in the process of creating solutions to problems or choices of activities and shared holidays.

BE CONSISTENT IN SETTING STANDARDS OF BEHAVIOUR

MAKE SURE THAT ALL ADULTS IN THE HOUSEHOLD AGREE ON THESE STANDARDS, TAKE PART IN THE DISCIPLINING, AND AGREE ON THE CONSEQUENCES. DISCIPLINE MUST BE CONSISTENT. DON'T LET YOUR CHILD GET AWAY WITH SOMETHING ONE DAY AND THEN PUNISH HIM FOR IT THE NEXT DAY.

Stepfamilies may go through different stages. Initially the union may begin with expectations to live happily every after. Then negative feelings such as guilt, jealousy and resentment creep in. Create an opportunity for the family to come together and express discontent or talk about problems they are experiencing,

During family sessions at home, everyone needs to be listened to. If these sessions aren't working, the first aim of family therapy is to enable each person to feel heard and understood.

It isn't easy to work things out, but it is worth the effort. If the children are not happy, this will have a detrimental effect on your new and often vulnerable second marriage. I suggest not rushing into marriage or moving in with your new partner. Your children may still be reeling from the after-effects of divorce. Give them an opportunity to gradually get to know your new partner so that there is a period of adjustment. This could span two to three years. Don't force the relationship.

Allow a connection to develop slowly between your partner and your children. Similarly, if your partner has children, give them the time and space to get to know you. I would also recommend being sure that you want to invest in the relationship on a long-term basis before you involve the children. This is important because children, especially young ones, can quickly form attachments to a new partner. They may then have to experience loss of this connection if you separate from the person.

So you have reached the stage when you want to make a commitment and move in together and/or marry. What should a couple be conscious of?

In merging two families, one of the big areas for potential conflict is the difference in values, culture, traditions and home rules. One family may be more conservative, with tighter discipline; the other may be more open, with less rigid rules.

Before you move in together, sit down with your partner and discuss these issues. It is vital that you are in agreement about how you will implement discipline and house rules. There is a strong tendency for the biological parent to defend his own child at all costs. Anyone who has lived in a blended family will know this.

We may not even like our stepchildren. I strongly advise against continuing the relationship if you cannot be at least fair and kind to your stepchildren. Prevention is the key. If you really do not like your stepchildren, think hard about moving in together. You don't have to love them, but you need to be prepared to treat them with respect and meet their needs. Remember, they have not chosen you. You chose their parent, and now they are forced to have you as an integral part of their life. So it's up to you to have the maturity to handle problems that arise with firmness and care.

Should a step-parent discipline her partner's child?

This depends on a number of factors: firstly, the age. If you have young children and stepchildren, this will necessitate much hands-on parenting. The woman especially, if she is doing the major share of nurturing, needs to be empowered enough to apply discipline.

If you have teenagers you may decide that each parent will deal with discipline issues with their own children. However, there would still need to be house rules that are respected by all. With younger children, sit down with your partner and discuss limits and consequences. With older children, include them in the discussion. This will make them feel involved and more likely to cooperate.

Children will model your behaviour. If you and your partner shout and yell at each other or them, sooner or later they will follow your example. Be aware of how you handle issues, and ensure that you and your partner present a united front.

What if you discover that you and your partner have totally opposite views on parenting?

Find a compromise that you can both live with. The children need to know and feel that family happiness is your highest priority. When you get together for discussions, brainstorm ideas. Try not to criticise each other's contribution. Give each person an opportunity to speak. Discuss the positives and negatives of each rule, and eliminate what will not work.

If both parents are working, explain to children that they all have to contribute to chores. Explain to them that by doing this, the family will have more fun time together. Establish clear rules and consequences. Don't have too many. Five is about right. These rules will depend on the age of the children and what the priorities are in the household. If the children are a similar age you can have the same rules. If they are different ages, the rules need to be made age-appropriate. For example, with school-age children the rules may be about chores, amount of television, bedtime, homework and pocket money. With teenagers they may be about curfew, smoking, alcohol, sex issues and financial support.

What are other factors to be aware of?

There is often a tendency to indulge or spoil children who have emerged from a divorce situation. This may be done out of guilt, as an attempt to compensate for the pain you may have caused your children. You may spoil your children in a game of one-upmanship with the other biological parent. This can create an imbalance in a blended family. Aim for fairness.

How do you ensure that each child gets treated equally?

It isn't always possible to be absolutely equal in terms of distribution of time, energy and resources. However, we often respond on a 'needs' basis. We look at each child as an individual and try to meet his special needs. This has to be done in a context of being fair to the others.

How do we handle financial issues in a blended family?

Again, there are many variables. Firstly, there are the obligations of each partner to their biological children, combined with the financial needs of the new family. Finances may be stretched running two households, and resentment may creep in.

Sit down with your partner and have a practical conversation around money. Look at your combined earnings, personal commitments, and your joint expenses. Work out and agree on a reasonable budget or allocation of funds. Depending on the age of the children, equalise pocket money or allowances as much as possible. Be realistic about what you expect from each other.

It is best not to interfere with what your partner is giving his own children as long as it doesn't compromise the family's needs. There are big decisions to be made; for example, do all children go to public or private schools? What if the child's other parent is in a different financial situation? Problems are likely to appear especially if there is poverty or extreme wealth.

Another issue is sharing time between your children, your partner's children and your new partner. How do we go about this to avoid jealousy and conflict?

By their father or mother remarrying, stepchildren will probably feel that their dream of their parents reconciling is finally shattered. The new step-parent can be perceived as the enemy, just by being part of the child's father or mother's life. As a step-parent, you don't have to have done anything negative to deserve this status. They now have to share their biological parent's time and love with you. They may be too young or immature to understand that love is not a finite thing.

Each parent should explain and stress that even though they have remarried, they still love and care about their biological children, just as much as they did before. Make sure you spend separate time with your children away from the new spouse. You can do this in a way that is not divisive. Have a regular meal out together or some ritual you can maintain.

What if the children fight and argue among themselves?

You can't force children to love their stepbrothers and sisters, but you can insist they treat each other with respect and civility. Often behaviour problems emerge when a child has her birth order changed. For example, a child who was the eldest sibling in her first family, enjoying certain privileges, is supplanted by an older stepsibling. The child has lost her special place in the family. The same goes for the youngest child, who may feel displaced.

Be aware of these possibilities and try to meet each child's need for love and attention. Don't, however, succumb to manipulation or victim mentality. If one of your children does manifest severe behaviour problems, get professional help. Try to find the underlying problem. Don't let the situation deteriorate. The earlier you intervene, the easier it will be to fix the problem. In general, children do need need time and understanding to adjust to their new family.

Who do you put first, your children or your mate?

Wherever possible, whether in a first or blended family, parents should put their relationship first but their children a close second. This gives the children a sense of security. When parents put children first, they can create a division in their relationship with each other, which invites the children to play one partner off against the other.

This is not an invitation to neglect children. Children should be treated with love, respect and care. If one partner is particularly selfish or demanding, children may suffer. There are times when a parent has to put a child's needs first, for example, if a child is ill or going through a crisis of sorts. If you think your partner is being unreasonable in her demands, go and see a therapist together.

TEACH YOUR CHILD EMPATHY

TEACH YOUR CHILD TO BE SENSITIVE TO THE NEEDS AND FEELINGS OF OTHERS. THINK OF THE THINGS YOU WOULD HAVE LIKED YOUR PARENTS TO SAY TO YOU AND DO WITH YOU. IF WE ARE AWARE OF WHAT WE ARE DOING WRONG, WE CAN LEARN FROM OUR MISTAKES. WE WILL GRADUALLY BECOME MORE RELAXED, MORE CONFIDENT, MORE IN CHARGE AND, ABOVE ALL, MORE EFFECTIVE AS PARENTS.

Do you have any examples of therapy benefiting a blended family?

I saw a couple recently – Clare had two sons, nine and seven. Christopher had two daughters, thirteen and fifteen. So the children were at different stages in their lives.

The girls were rude to their stepmother and refused to cooperate. She found it extremely upsetting, and had difficulty in managing the situation. The girls felt powerless as they felt they did not have any say in the new arrangement. The rebellious behaviour of the two girls was masking their pain. Pain is often expressed as anger.

We had a number of sessions together. I established the first rule. Everyone had to talk to each other the way they wanted that person to talk to them. Next they were invited to participate in structuring the rules and consequences. I made sure that everyone had the opportunity to express his or her thoughts and feelings, and that everyone felt listened to and heard. There was then less need to express anger outside of therapy. I also helped the family improve their communication skills and increase respect among family members.

Gradually the situation improved. As my client did not have her own daughters, she began to enjoy doing special activities with them, and a bond slowly formed. Her husband also forged a relationship with his partner's sons by doing simple fun things such as ball games and rough and tumble activities. In this case, the gender differences worked as a benefit.

Each step-family has its own particular dynamics, with issues that need to be resolved. It is often a complex situation exacerbated by intense emotions. Going into a blended family with eyes wide open may help you both anticipate some of the problems and deal with them more effectively.

Toolbox

- Show your children a confident attitude that indicates you will work out the difficulties.
- Maintain a united front with your partner.
- Involve the children in establishing routines for outings and chores.
- Both parents should administer discipline when needed. By preventing one from having input, you render them powerless. Make it clear to all the children that both parents should be treated with respect.
- Don't be afraid of discussing thorny issues with each other, such as finances and discipline.
- Maintain a sense of humour and don't be oversensitive
- Be prepared to learn from your mistakes.
- Patience improves harmony in a blended family.
- Come up with a set of rules and regulations.
- Have five important house rules to start with. You can add more or adjust the ones that do not work later.
- Have the long-range goal of creating a happy and harmonious family. This may help you get through the difficult stages.
- A good idea is to have one room that is off limits for the children, a sanctuary for you and your partner. This may be a shared study or bedroom.
- Maintain intimacy with your partner.

- If possible, give each child their own room. You may have to divide a room in two to achieve this. Personal space gives children a sense of belonging and security.
- Allow children to negotiate with one another about issues such as television programs, computer time and other shared resources.
- Remember, in all situations, two wrongs don't make a right. Step-parents should demonstrate wisdom and maturity as adults.
- If a child becomes aggressive or angry, find out why he is angry. He may be hurting.

Conclusion

I SPOKE WITH JO, AGED twenty-three, who provided the inspiration behind *The Pocket Therapist*. She began therapy at the age of eighteen. After two years of therapy, she had transformed her life. Here is her story.

When I was eighteen, I went through a period when I was sad and depressed. My parents had divorced, my father was remarried and the family had been moved around a lot. There was a lot of pain and anger in me. My mum decided I should have therapy to help me overcome my negative state of mind. We opened the Yellow Pages. I chose Susie Wise because I really liked her name. I felt with a name like Wise I couldn't go wrong.

I liked Susie immediately. I believe that everything happens for a reason. The first day I went to see her was a life-changing experience. You don't meet a lot of people who change your life, so I felt very lucky that I had found a good therapist.

I made a commitment to see her every week. I put my heart and soul into the therapy. I went to each session armed with a notebook, and after two years I filled up volumes. I kept all my notes so that I could go back to them when issues resurfaced.

I believe that if you want to make the most of your life, you need the tools to handle situations as they arise. Before I had therapy I didn't really know myself. I didn't understand who I was. I've never had anything terrible happen in my life, like rape or abuse, but I was struggling to find my own identity.

When I began therapy I didn't tell anyone except my mum, not even my best friend. Later I shared my experiences, but while I was in therapy, I kept my sessions confidential. I felt safe and secure doing this. I got myself an education for life that can never be substituted. Through therapy I came to believe that anything was possible. I achieved a level of independence and became more assertive. I learnt how to ask for help from Susie, and how to give help to others. I know how to treat people. At a young age, I have learnt the skills to be a manager. This has helped my career and enabled me to make rapid progress. I feel I have a lifetime guarantee in the skills I have learnt.

I have always been a deep thinker. This is what led me into a downward spiral initially. I'm so happy that I chose to go to therapy. I asked myself, 'What's the worst that can happen? I may cry a bit, maybe it won't work, but there is nothing to lose'.

Since completing therapy I have had to deal with some challenging and painful events, including the death of my godfather last year. That was the worst thing that ever happened to me, as I was very close to him. I now miss him dreadfully, but I felt I coped with this tragedy well, as the therapy has given me the tools to manage my grief.

If you can afford it, I encourage anyone to invest in themselves by finding a good therapist and making a commitment to go. You need to go regularly over a reasonable period of time to get results. I invite you to have a life-changing experience. You cannot learn these skills at school or university. The knowledge and emotional rewards are very satisfying.

Today I'm a much happier, more confident and outgoing person. I have better relationships, a successful career and I'm at peace with myself.

Therapy can indeed change your life. For many people, it is a wonderful release to be able to bare their souls to a person who cares but is unbiased. As the therapist will never judge you, you can be totally honest, admitting to feelings that you perhaps cannot face telling anyone else. In being able to open up, therapy maximises your potential to grow.

Appendix

RELATIONSHIPS

- Relationships Australia 02 9418 8800. Freecall outside Sydney 1300 364 277.
- Centacare Relationship Counselling 02 9283 4899.
- Domestic Violence Line 1800 656 463
- Lifeline 13 11 14 statewide.

DRUGS/ALCOHOL

- Alcohol and Drug Information 1800 422 599
- Al-anon 02 9264 9255 (24 hours)
- Drug Advice 02 9332 8777

PARENTING

- Parent Line 13 20 55. For advice and information for parents with children up to 18 years of age.
- Family Planning 02 9716 6099.
- Tresillian 02 9787 0800/8300/2124. 24-hour Parenting Helpline 9787 5255. Information and counselling for parents or carers of children under five years (24-hour); Also Karitane 02 9794 1852. Hotline 1800 677 961.
- Family Support Services Association 02 9743 6565.
- Parenting website www.community.nsw.gov.au
- Feeding/Breastfeeding 02 9639 8686
- Parent Support 02 9212 3244
- Single Lone Parents 02 9251 5622
- Playgroup Association 02 9604 5513

- Financial Counselling Service 1800 808 488
- NSW Rape Crisis Centre 1800 424 017
- Drug Advice 02 9332 8777
- NSW Women's Refuge Resource Centre 02 9518 8379
- Sudden Infant Death 1800 651 186

CHILD WELFARE
- Child Abuse 1800 688 009 (24 hours)
- National Child Care Access Hotline 1800 670 305

WOMEN'S WELFARE
- NSW Rape Crisis Centre 1800 424 017
- NSW Women's Refuge Resource Centre 02 9518 8379

MISCELLANEOUS
- Legal Aid 1800 806 913
- Mental Health 02 9816 1611
- Compassionate Friends (Bereavement) 02 9290 2355

Recommended Reading

Beecher, Sabine, *Happiness, It's Up To You*, Collins Dove, Melbourne, 1988.

Bolton, Robert, *People Skills*, Simon & Schuster, Sydney, 1987.

Brandon, Nathanial, *Six Pillars Of Self-Esteem*, Bantam Books, New York, 1994.

Cappello, Dominic & Schwartz, Pepper, *Ten Talks Parents Must Have With Their Children About Sex and Character*, Hypersion, New York, 2000.

Cleese, John & Skynner, Robyn, *Families & How To Survive Them*, Methuen, London, 1983

Colling, Terry & Vickers, Janet, *Teenagers – A Guide To Understanding Them*, Bantam, Sydney, Australia, 1988.

Hart, Dr Louise & Orr, Dr Fred, *The Winning Family: Increasing Self-Esteem In Your Children and Yourself*, Hutchinson, Sydney, 1987

Davitz, Lois & Joel, *How To Live Almost Happily With A Teenager*, Dove Communications, Melbourne, 1982.

Mary Heineman, *Losing Your Shirt*, Hazelden, Minnesota, USA, 1992.

Levett, Jan & Toms, Laraine, *Positive Parenting*, Nelson Publishers, Melbourne, 1985.

McGraw, Dr Phillip N C, *Relationship Rescue*. Hyperion, New York, 2000.

McGraw, Dr Phillip N C, *Life Strategies*, Ebury Press Vermillion, London, 1999.

Sanders, Mathew R, *Every Parent. A Positive Approach To Children's Behaviour*, Addison-Wesley Publishing, Sydney, 1992.

Schnarch, David, *Passionate Marriage*, Scribe Publications, USA, 1997.

Seigel, Eleonor, & Siegel, Linda, *Keys To Disciplining Your Child*, Barrons Educational Series, New York, 1993.

Severe, Sal, *How To Behave So Your Children Will, Too*, Viking (Penguin), New York, 2000.

Coleman, Dr Paul. *The 30 Secrets of Happily Married Couples*, Bob Adams Inc. Publishers, USA, 1992.

Downing Orr, Dr Kristina, *What to Do if You Are Burnt Out and Blue*, Thorsons, London, 2000.

Kubler Ross, *Elizabeth, Death – The Final Stage of Growth*, Prentice Hall, New Jersey, USA, 1975.

Lindenfeld, Gael, *Managing Anger*, Thorsons, London, 1993.

McNamara, Lynne & Mornson, Jennifer, *Separation, Divorce and After*, University of Queensland Press, 1982.

Montgomery, Dr Bob & Evans, Lynette, *You and Stress*, Penguin Books, Australia, 1984.

Schwartz, Morrie, *Letting Go: Reflections on Living while Dying*, Pan Books, New York, 1996.

Tanner, Susan & Ball, Jillian, *Beating the Blues*, Doubleday, Sydney, 1989.

Twerski, Rabbi Abraham J, *Getting Up When You Are Down*, Shaar Press, New York, 1997.

Van Praagh, James, *Healing Grief*, Hodder, Sydney, Australia, 2000.

Index